BOLLIN
Valley PAST & PRESENT

BOLLIN Valley PAST & PRESENT

Keith Warrender

Willow PUBLISHING

Quarry Bank Mill, Styal.

Text copyright ©Keith Warrender 2016
Photographs ©Keith Warrender 2016 unless acknowledged
First published 2016 by Willow Publishing

Willow Publishing
36 Moss Lane, Timperley,
Altrincham, Cheshire WA15 6SZ

ISBN 978-0-946361-46-5

Book designed by Keith Warrender
Printed by the Buxton Press

Dedicated to Edward Daniel Warrender

Front cover: Wilmslow Park
Opposite title page: Dunham Massey
Title page: Footpath near Vicar Farm, Wilmslow

The Bollin Valley Way near Newton Hall Farm, Mottram St Andrew.

CONTENTS

The River Bollin rises here in a field at Macclesfield Forest.

INTRODUCTION

The Axe and Cleaver, Dunham.

Here is another selection of people and places in the Bollin Valley. It's about things not covered in the first book 'Bollin Valley from Macclesfield to the Ship canal' but in some instances I have returned with new information on subjects previously mentioned. The book is not just confined to things immediately beside the river, it takes in features of interest within easy walking distance. People have commented how much they discovered about the area from my book, and it's my hope that this new work will contain more revelations. I was surprised by what I found in my research for the second volume and I hope you will be too.

I am most grateful to the many people who have allowed me access to photograph their homes and provided valuable information about properties which remain hidden behind high walls and hedges. The book contains the histories of many notable halls, houses and businesses throughout the valley, revealing the successes and sometimes tragedies and failures of their owners. If you can provide further information about the families who lived there, I should be pleased to hear from you.

I know of people who have used the first book as a guide to walking along the valley, and I hope this second volume will provide further inspiration to explore this beautiful valley which is so rich in heritage and natural life.

I should like to emphasise that the maps in the book are purely approximate guides to the locations of places in the valley. They are not of uniform scale and Ordnance Survey maps should always be used for footpaths and detailed road networks.

The book is also a record of many 'lost' places - the RAF camp at Wilmslow, Dunham's PoW camp, the halls at Tytherington and the Wilmslow Grange estate. It's about some of the characters of the district - 'Jarmug' of Wilmslow, the great Macclesfield historian Walter Smith and Francis Godlee of Stamford Lodge whose time-keeping was legendary. The valley has not been immune to great engineering projects, and the extensive construction workings of Trentabank Reservoir at Macclesfield Forest, the massive Manchester Airport Runway project which transformed that particular part of the valley, and the dramatic undertaking of the Warburton High Level Bridge over the Ship Canal, are all covered here.

But if you simply like to enjoy the peace and quiet of the riverside walks and the surrounding countryside, you will find that reflected in the many photographs I have taken especially for this book. Once again, producing the book has been a great adventure and during the preparation I have met many interesting people who have been so enthusiastic in sharing what they know. This is a thirty-mile long valley so if you can't find what you're looking for either in this or my previous book, or if you have a favourite place not already mentioned, please let me know. I hope that for many, the photographs will provide reminiscences for those who live away from the valley or who cannot visit it. Whatever your interest, I hope you enjoy this fresh look at the Bollin Valley.

Keith Warrender

Overleaf: Looking towards Macclesfield Forest and Shutlingslow from Tegg's Nose Country Park.

Red Campion beside the Bollin at Bowdon.

Footpath near Langley Hall.

The Bollin valley from Prestbury, with the Kerridge Hills in the distance.

MACCLESFIELD FOREST

Domesday Book records the area as a notable woodland but gradual enclosure for cultivation, over the centuries, left it with few trees. By 1795 Aitkin in his description of the area called it 'a naked and dreary track', and wrote of the lawlessness here with the activities of the 'flash-men' hawkers who cheated their suppliers, then established themselves as farmers. Also roaming the area were the 'Broken Cross gang' who fooled people with their 'thimble-rigging tricks', but were later jailed. Even in 1850, a local directory describes the area as 'cold, bleak and mountainous, and very unproductive.'

When it became a Royal Forest, the Sovereign had rights over the water in these hills. Then in 1685 Macclesfield was granted permission to convey piped water from various wells and springs in these 'waste lands'. An Enclosure Act of 1796 gave further powers to extract water from more of its streams. As Macclesfield's

10

prosperity grew so it required increasing amounts of water to satisfy the needs of the silk industry and its residents, with eventually four reservoirs being built. The River Bollin rises on the edge of the Forest in a field opposite Toothill House. It is referred to as Bollin Brook on OS maps as it flows through the forest into Trentabank Reservoir.

Today, the forest still contains the remains of a number of old farms which preceded it. Ironically the farms that survived up to the 1930s did not have piped water despite the nearness of the great reservoirs. The 1830s Tithe Map shows there were about eleven farms there, which increased further during the nineteenth century.

The present-day forest was begun in 1930 when Macclesfield Corporation announced that 400 acres were to be covered with 800,000 trees. It was expected to take five years and would provide protection for the reservoirs and water-gathering grounds. Trees would keep away cattle and other animals which could cause bacterial infection, and keep the waters cool, reducing evaporation.

The forest was to contain Japanese Larch, Corsican Pine, Norway Spruce, Sitka Spruce and Black Poplar. The soil had been tested and was found to be ideal for planting. The Corporation hoped that within thirty years they would recoup part of their outlay by selling some of the trees for posts or mining pit-props. The first saplings were planted by the mayor and some of the councillors in the early stage which involved the planting of about 123,000 trees over 86 acres. A nursery was established for seedlings to be grown before they were planted in the forest. The cost of the scheme was about £5,500 with support from the Forestry Commission.

Today the forest has expanded to 988 acres and is owned by United Utilities. Two thirds of the forest to the east, are within the Peak

National Park. In 1933, the Ridgegate Reservoir was emptied in order to carry out reconstruction work on the embankment and the valves. However the following year there was a drought and in early September permission was given by Lord Derby for water to be pumped from his land at Clough Brook to the east of the forest. Half a mile of piping was laid over Standing Stone to the streams which fed the reservoir which only had seven days' supply left. The brook which had its source close to the Cat and Fiddle Inn provided about 300,000 gallons a day. There were emergency plans to use the Bottoms Reservoir, if necessary, which provided compensation water to the River Bollin.

People in the Hurdsfield district of Macclesfield whose water came from a spring at Kerridge had to rely briefly on supplies brought in barrels by cart. Residents had to be convinced the temporary supplies were fit to drink by the carriers, who said it was as good as ice-cream and drank it at each stop to prove it was safe.

Ridgegate Reservoir and Leather's Smithy Pub.

The Foresters

Robert Tebay was Reservoir Keeper for 38 years until 1929 when Michael Burke took over the role. Burke had been in charge of the pipe-laying between the reservoirs and Macclesfield and lived in the bungalow (since demolished) overlooking Trentabank Reservoir. John Hambleton remembers, when a boy, taking eggs to Burke who generously gave him half a crown. Michael Burke's son Tom took over after his retirement in 1948 and became Head Forester. His duties also included responsibility for the maintenance of Ridgegate Filter Works, and analysis of the water quality at the Langley reservoirs. He was transferred from Macclesfield Corporation to the Macclesfield District Water Board when it was established in 1960.

The work entailed fencing off areas, thinning the smaller trees and sawing them up to make into pit-props and fencing stakes. The forestry men also worked at Longdendale, Lyme Park and Goyt Valley.

Tom Burke (left) with Wilf Slack and Wilf Read cutting stakes 1951.

United Utilities

Wilf Slack

Wilf Slack (on left of photo) worked in the Forest for 34 years. His duties included tractor driving, and he had been acting Head Forester for eight months following the death of Tom Burke. During Wilf's time at the forest, four red deer were introduced into the forest from Lyme Park.

At his retirement in 1984, he was presented with a 'cattle crush' which steadied the cattle during injections and other treatments and inspections. This was to be used on his 60-acre farm which he and his wife ran. Wilf earlier worked at Windyway quarry - see page 32.

Forestry officer Bernard Annikin (right) had trained to be an accountant in the family firm but changed careers. His previous position had been as Head Forester for the Earl of Seafield in Scotland. He insisted his workers addressed him as 'Mr Annikin'.

When he died in 1971, his duties were divided between Mr A Anderton who was in charge of the water and Mr Bailey who managed the Forest. Bernard Annikin became the new Forestry Officer in 1975 taking over the management of the 1000 acres of forest and over half a million trees for the North West Water Authority which had succeeded the Macclesfield District Water Board. He regarded the Forest as providing a service to the community, including fishing facilities in its four reservoirs, a venue for spaniel trials, fox shoots, and habitats for bird lovers to observe the grebes, herons and kingfishers.

The Forest was run as a business, with trees felled and cut at the Authority's own saw mill to make about 700 pit-props and fence posts a week. The sale of Christmas trees also helped the Forest to pay its way. Along with his foreman Wilf Slack, there were nine other forestry workers. Although the work could be tough in winter, the forest workers enjoyed the variety of work and being outdoors, experiencing the change of seasons.

Access Problems

When part of the Macclesfield Forest became part of the newly-formed Peak National Park in 1951, there were disagreements between the Park Authority and Macclesfield Corporation. The latter were unhappy with the wider access given to the public within the Forest.

In one weekend in June of that year the Macclesfield Borough Engineer reported that 800 visitors had descended on the area, trespassing in the afforested area, picnicing and sunbathing, bathing in the water used for public supply and parking a caravan for a weekend's stay.

When asked to leave, people said they thought they were entitled to do these things in a National Park. The Engineer expressed his concern over water pollution and the fire risk and the difficulties of providing enough people to patrol the Forest.

Let others sing of 'stately Thames'
Or 'banks and braes o'bonnie Doon'
I love to hear this Forest brook
In winter wild or leafy June
The babbling brook o' Bollin

From 'Bollin Brook' by Walter Smith

Walter Smith

Smith was well-known and respected for his writings on the people and countryside around Macclesfield as well as his service to the community. He worked as a railway engine driver but his real love was the history of the surrounding hills and villages, and at his retirement after almost fifty years with the railways in 1937, he devoted himself to researching and exploring the area. It also gave him time to set himself a new challenge - to teach himself Greek, Latin and Hebrew in order to understand old manuscripts.

Well-known

His love of the countryside began when he stayed at Rose's Farm, Langley at the time of the First World War. He was a familiar figure in the locality, described as tall and distinguished, with a 'hawk-like' look, striding out into the countryside. He regularly contributed articles to the local newspaper and wrote 'Over the Hills Near Macclesfield' published in 1921. Friends said he was an engaging walking companion because of his immense, almost encyclopedic, knowledge of the locality which was always delivered in his distinctive, clear voice. He was always willing to help anyone whether friend or stranger with local history queries.

Although it was perhaps in the hills where he felt most at home, he was also active as a local Macclesfield councillor for nine years during which he was a member of the Water Committee. His interest in local history enabled him to research into water regulations back to the 17th century. Unsurprisingly, he campaigned for walkers' rights and preservation of the countryside, but was also a fund-raiser for a cancer relief charity.

He was a devoted member of the Unitarian chapel on King Edward Street Macclesfield, and with his knowledge of the past was able to obtain deeds connected with the chapel from the Brocklehurst family. He is said to have spent many long and happy hours poring over the old documents.

Beginnings

Walter Smith was born in 1872 in Macclesfield, the son of Isaac, a silk weaver from Bickerstaffe near Ormskirk who died when Walter was eight. He had two brothers - Henry Pimm Smith, a Salvation Army officer, and Fred who had a greengrocer's on Mill Lane Macclesfield. His sister Alice Ann and her husband, John Ashworth, were both cotton weavers. He started work aged twelve at a cotton mill then later worked at the Brocklehurst silk mill. From there he was a cleaner and fireman at the Gorton Tank Works Manchester before becoming an engine driver on the LNER until his retirement at the age of 65.

Walter and his wife Ellen had two daughters - Alice, a self employed silk machinist, and Doris, a school teacher. At the time of his death in 1949, Walter and family were living at Blakelow Road which looked across Macclesfield, as well as having glorious views over his beloved hills and moors.

Memorial

In view of his work and service to the area, it had been suggested he should receive the freedom of Macclesfield. But while he never formally received this award, he had certainly enjoyed the pleasures and freedom of the countryside around Macclesfield for many years. After his death there were discussions on how they could honour his achievements, and in March 1951 it was announced

Macclesfield Museums

The Walter Smith memorial near Standing Stone.

United Utilities

This page and opposite, the countryside which Walter Smith knew so well.

that a memorial was to be set up close to Standing Stone at an appropriately peaceful site overlooking the hills, the Forest and the towering Shuttlingslow. Subscriptions were requested for both the memorial and the formation of a collection of Smith's writings and other local history books for Macclesfield Library.

At a ceremony on 12th May 1951, the boulder with an inscription on a brass plate was unveiled by Smith's two daughters. Amongst the 150 people present were the Mayor of Macclesfield and representatives of Macclesfield and District Field Club of which Smith was an original member. Walter Smith's old friend, Thomas Abraham JP, gave a speech in which he said that Smith was a man with great gifts and had given them unsparingly to his home town. After the ceremony there was a service of dedication conducted by the minister from Macclesfield Unitarian Chapel.

Doris Smith sent in a letter of thanks to the local paper for the support for the memorial to her father. She wrote that during the service of dedication she could hear a curlew singing above the sun-bathed hills and felt that here was peace and a rich fulfilment of a long and useful life. Smith was an enthusiast of Burns' poetry hence the line on the plaque 'We climb the hills thegither'. Some years ago, the original brass memorial attached to the stone was stolen. The original wording has now been carved into the boulder. The Walter Smith collection is available at Macclesfield Library and further items at Chester County Archives.

Standing Stone

The Walter Smith memorial is close to the top of Dark Lane where it is known as Standing Stone.

Locals believed the summit of the crossroads was once the burial site for local suicides. They were interred without religious ceremony and a wooden stake driven through the coffinless body. They would be also hanged on a gibbet. Possibly it was also the last resting place of people who had broken the old Forest laws. Unsurprisingly, locals avoided travelling past this spot at night time.

The 1873 OS map shows a Standing Stone Farm nearby. Also, on the track to Ferriser Farm, the former site of an old cross is marked.

Walter Smith wrote that there was a large granite stone embedded in the ground just inside a gateway by the roadside.

Macclesfield Forest Chapel

Countryside to the south-east of Macclesfield Forest, towards Shutlingsloe.

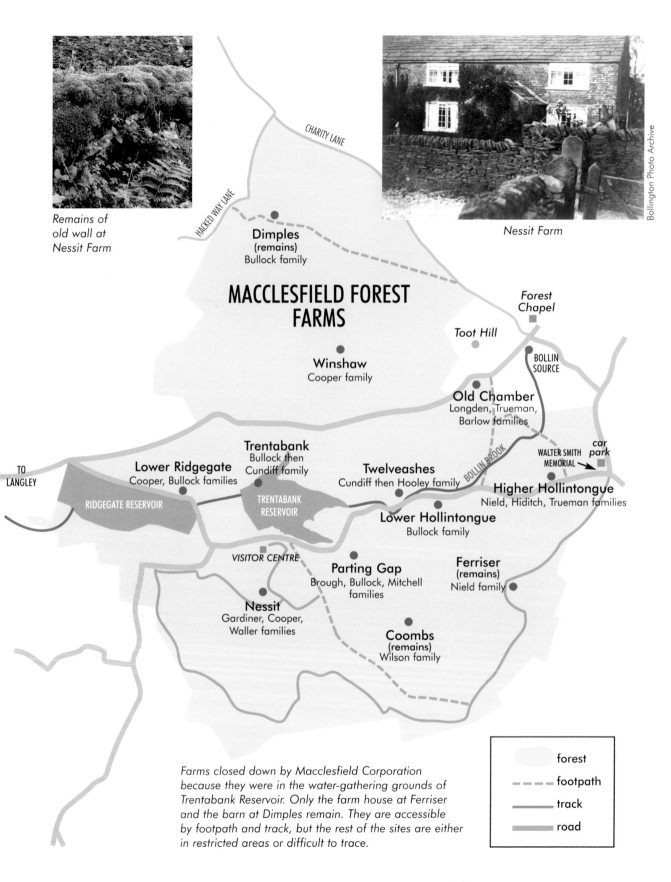

Remains of old wall at Nessit Farm

Nessit Farm

Bollington Photo Archive

CHARITY LANE

HACKED WAY LANE

Dimples
(remains)
Bullock family

MACCLESFIELD FOREST FARMS

Forest Chapel

Toot Hill

BOLLIN SOURCE

Winshaw
Cooper family

Old Chamber
Longden, Trueman,
Barlow families

BOLLIN BROOK

Trentabank
Bullock then
Cundiff family

Twelveashes
Cundiff then Hooley family

car park

WALTER SMITH
MEMORIAL

TO
LANGLEY

Lower Ridgegate
Cooper, Bullock families

RIDGEGATE RESERVOIR

TRENTABANK
RESERVOIR

Higher Hollintongue
Nield, Hiditch, Trueman families

Lower Hollintongue
Bullock family

VISITOR CENTRE

Parting Gap
Brough, Bullock, Mitchell
families

Ferriser
(remains)
Nield family

Nessit
Gardiner, Cooper,
Waller families

Coombs
(remains)
Wilson family

Farms closed down by Macclesfield Corporation because they were in the water-gathering grounds of Trentabank Reservoir. Only the farm house at Ferriser and the barn at Dimples remain. They are accessible by footpath and track, but the rest of the sites are either in restricted areas or difficult to trace.

	forest
- - - -	footpath
———	track
▬▬▬	road

Lost farms of Macclesfield Forest

The farms around the Forest and Wildboarclough date back to the early 1600s when the rigid laws of the Royal Forest eased and the land was cultivated and farms established.

In the 1920s Macclesfield Corporation began to purchase the farms to make way for afforestation. It cost the Corporation over £20,000 for the purchase of 1000 acres of land within the watershed area. The Earl of Derby owned many of the farms - Dimples, Top Close, Winshaw, Twelveashes, Higher and Lower Hollintongue, Parting Gap, Ferriser, Trentabank and Coombs and they were purchased for £19,000 in 1924.

Most of the farms were still tenanted up to 1931 and had been held by the same families for decades. Some were used as temporary accommodation by the reservoir constructors. The local council continued to buy farm land around the Forest in the 1950s for use as water-gathering grounds.

Dimples Farm was so named because it was sited in a hollow in the slope of the hill. As well as the farmstead, there used to be a large red-bricked barn. The Bullock family had farmed here since at least the early 1800s. The initials JB 1880 on the barn refer to James Bullock who was in occupation until about 1892.

It was reported in 1864 that Francis Bullock who farmed here for over twenty years had a two and a half-year old sow who had given birth to a litter of 25 piglets. In previous litters she'd had up to 18.

Left: Cluster of buildings at Dimples Farm c1870.

Ferriser Farm before the property was bought by Macclesfield Corporation to be part of the Forest area.

Ferriser (or Ferresaw) Farm was occupied by James and Sarah Nield by 1828. Their son John who took over the farm lived there until his death in 1879 aged 82 and was buried at Forest Chapel. The Nields continued to farm here through William, Joseph, Jabez and his son of the same name until 1931. The remains of the farm still exist.

The site of Trentabank Farm (opposite page) is now below Trentabank Reservoir. It was referred to as 'Trenthambank' on the 1875 OS map. The River Bollin ('Bollin Brook') can just be seen in the foreground, along with Trenthambank Wood in the background to the right.

The farm had been in the hands of the Bullock family until it was taken over by the Cundiffs by 1881. Barbara Bullock (nee Cundiff) who grew up on the farm remembered how a dead relative was 'laid out' in the little room which extended at the back of the farm.

Work began to demolish Trentabank Farm on Friday 16 November 1928. Most of the stonework was re-used in the initial breaching of the north-east side of the reservoir between the overflow shaft and the approach bridge to the valve tower. The weather had been exceptionally bad but the demolition work was completed in three weeks.

John Hambleton

Trentabank Farm

United Utilities

Trentabank Farm during the reservoir construction.

In 1891, Lower Ridgegate Farm - by Ridgegate Reservoir, was being farmed by William Bullock. He had previously been at Parting Gate Farm. His son Fred was the last tenant who left before the building of Trentabank Reservoir. However the property was being let as a furnished cottage in 1914.

The bungalow overlooking Trentabank Reservoir, originally home of the Resident Engineer.

*Dr Herbert Lapworth,
eminent geologist
and water engineer*

Engineer Stanley R Bate

Trentabank Reservoir

By 1912, Macclesfield needed an additional reservoir to the three Langley Reservoirs to meet the growing manufacturing and domestic needs as well as providing compensation water to the River Bollin. After much heated argument it was decided that Trentabank was the only feasible scheme which could supply a further 465,000 gallons of water daily. An Act was passed in 1923 enabling the Corporation to purchase land and materials at an estimated cost of £188,600.

The Reservoir covered Dark Lane, the old road between Leather's Smithy and Trentabank Farm, and the route of the River Bollin. Dr Herbert Lapworth was appointed as the Engineer, and Stanley R Bate the Resident Engineer. 200 local men were employed on the scheme and brought in daily by specially-provided North Western buses from Macclesfield. The work involved the construction of an embankment, a pipeline to Macclesfield, various shafts and a half-mile road diversion. Millstone Grit stone for the road and most of the reservoir works was extracted from Nessit Quarry.

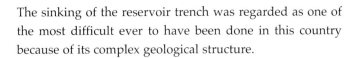

The sinking of the reservoir trench was regarded as one of the most difficult ever to have been done in this country because of its complex geological structure.

In March 1924 work began on the new road followed by preliminary work on the 73ft-high embankment in June. The Bollin was diverted through a tunnel under the bank in 1925. The work was undertaken as a municipal scheme rather than by a private contractor. This proved a wise decision as there were a number of unforeseen problems during construction that would have required the drawing-up of new contracts. The main problem was the discovery of unstable sand beneath the embankment foundations and it took a further three years to complete. It was a challenging project, and Herbert Lapworth later admitted that he and his deputy used to whistle on site to disguise their true feelings of anxiety.

The more skilled workers such as the loco men 'the black gang', fitters and blacksmiths, boarded at Prospect Farm which was formerly known as Lower Hollingtongue. Trentabank Farm was the temporary home of the works foreman or 'walking ganger'. Engineer Stanley Bate lodged at a specially-built timber bungalow overlooking the reservoir workings near Nessit. Parting Gap and Coombs Farms were used to house Corporation workmen after the farms became vacant in 1926.

Drinking water was first pumped into Macclesfield on 17th July 1929 before the Reservoir was officially opened on 2nd October 1929 by the Duke of Gloucester, with an estimated 6,000 people present. The finished cost had risen to £215,000, but the reservoir gave an extra 100 days' water supply to Macclesfield. Before opening the valve which symbolically released the water into the town, the Duke said in his speech that there was an urgent demand throughout the country to have at least one bathroom in every house. Earlier in the day he had opened extensions to Macclesfield Infirmary.

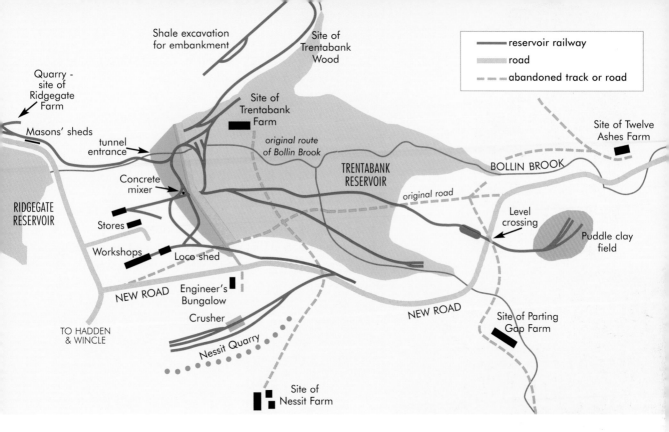

Map labels:

Shale excavation for embankment

Site of Trentabank Wood

Quarry - site of Ridgegate Farm

Masons' sheds

Site of Trentabank Farm

tunnel entrance

original route of Bollin Brook

Site of Twelve Ashes Farm

BOLLIN BROOK

TRENTABANK RESERVOIR

Concrete mixer

RIDGEGATE RESERVOIR

original road

Level crossing

Stores

Puddle clay field

Workshops

Loco shed

Engineer's Bungalow

NEW ROAD

Crusher

NEW ROAD

Nessit Quarry

Site of Parting Gap Farm

TO HADDEN & WINCLE

Site of Nessit Farm

Legend:
— reservoir railway
road
- - - abandoned track or road

Reservoir railway

For the construction of the reservoir, a narrow-gauge railway was built to carry building material from quarries, shale sites and clay pit. Stone was also imported from nearby quarries by lorries.

Five internal combustion locomotives were used on the 2ft-gauge track. There were inevitably mishaps on the hilly site. A loco buried itself into the bank below the bungalow, another smashed through the crossing gates on the new road, and a driverless runaway loco ran through the engine shed and ended up in the smithy.

One of the first Sentinel locomotives came off the rails twenty-four times during the first day. Another Sentinel engine went out of control down an incline before its wheels locked and derailed and began vigorously rocking. The frightened driver refused to work on the site afterwards. After the reservoir was completed, two of the locomotives were used on various schemes around Hastings.

Avenue of trees planted in dedication to members of Macclesfield Council in 1931 at the beginning of tree planting in the Forest.

Valve tower, Trentabank Reservoir.

The route of the reservoir railway to the right of the stream before it entered the tunnel under the dam embankment. The line went to Ridgegate Quarry by the side of Ridgegate Reservoir seen in the background.

John Hambleton

Left: Trentabank was a local beauty spot with its displays of rhododendrons and lupins.

Below: Castellated hut by the Reservoir used by the Air Raid Precautions service during WWII.

John Hambleton

Trentabank has a heronry and nature reserve

The rush-bearing service used to attract large crowds.

Wilf Slack

Macclesfield Forest Chapel

The hamlet of Macclesfield Forest has a chapel, two farms, and the former school and school house. The chapel's stone altar pedestal is unusual for these parts, and it is speculated it may pre-date the building, possibly coming from the private Royal Chapel belonging to the nearby Chamber in the Forest which was to be seen on 18th century maps.

St Stephen's Chapel is famous for its annual rush-bearing service which originates from the practice of replacing the rushes used to provide warmth and comfort on the bare floor. The service remains an important date in the calendar for the people of the area as well as many visitors; although attendances are not as great as in years gone by when big crowds attended the ceremony. The day was treated as a holiday and there used to be gingerbread stalls outside the Chapel gates. Farm servants wore new boots given by their employers and it was an occasion of heavy drinking. In 1906, about a thousand people were expected to attend the open-air service.

The ancient pedestal supporting the altar slab can just be seen behind the decorated altar rail.

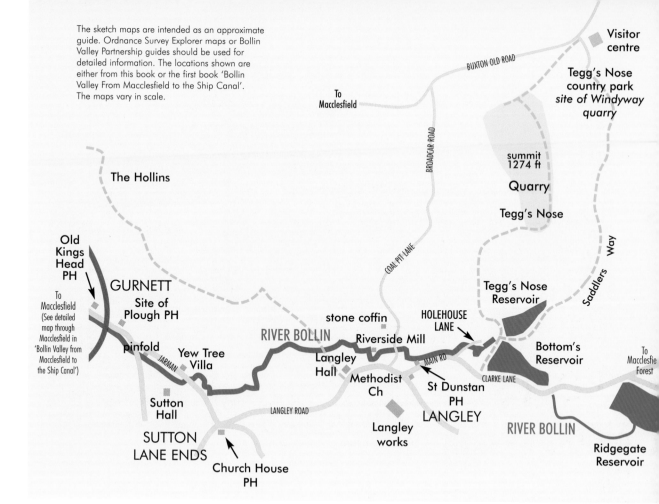

The sketch maps are intended as an approximate guide. Ordnance Survey Explorer maps or Bollin Valley Partnership guides should be used for detailed information. The locations shown are either from this book or the first book 'Bollin Valley From Macclesfield to the Ship Canal'. The maps vary in scale.

BUXTON OLD ROAD

To Macclesfield

BROADCAR ROAD

The Hollins

Visitor centre

Tegg's Nose country park *site of Windyway quarry*

summit 1274 ft

Quarry

Tegg's Nose

COAL PIT LANE

Saddlers Way

Old Kings Head PH

To Macclesfield (See detailed map through Macclesfield in 'Bollin Valley from Macclesfield to the Ship Canal')

GURNETT

Site of Plough PH

pinfold

JARMAN

Yew Tree Villa

stone coffin

RIVER BOLLIN

Riverside Mill

Langley Hall

Methodist Ch

HOLEHOUSE LANE

MAIN RD

St Dunstan PH

LANGLEY

CLARKE LANE

Tegg's Nose Reservoir

Bottom's Reservoir

To Macclesfie Forest

Sutton Hall

LANGLEY ROAD

Langley works

RIVER BOLLIN

SUTTON LANE ENDS

Church House PH

Ridgegate Reservoir

Tegg's Nose

31

Windyway Quarry

The old quarry is now the site of Tegg's Nose Country Park Visitor's Centre, cafe and car park. Wilf Slack (see page 15) became an apprentice stone-dresser here at 16. He made kerbs and sets at the quarry which produced a grey or blue-tinted stone and also used for monuments. It was cut from the quarry in 'logs' and transported to Bollington to be sawn up. A mechanical 'rock-getter crane' extracted rock from the ground.

Wilf used hammer and wedges to cut up the stone. He made five kerbs a day, whereas the more experienced workers finished eight daily. They worked in open-fronted sheds but if it was too cold and frosty it was impossible to work the stone. He was paid 16s a week at a time of much unemployment. There was no water on the site so it had to be fetched from a local farm. Nor were there any toilets.

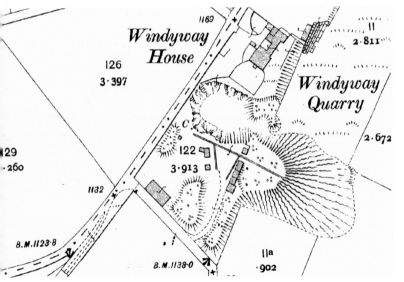

The quarry on 1910 map was in operation by 1895.

He started work at 7.30am, working until 7.30pm in the summer. He wore hiking boots, overalls, and a leather jacket to keep out the cold. Everyone realised the potential health dangers from the dust, but no protection was provided. A doctor regularly visited the site where it is known that four men in nine years had to be laid off after getting silicosis.

Wilf went home for his lunch at Crooked Yard Farm; others had theirs at the quarry office. It was officially a half-hour break, but often he was sent to the Setter Dog pub at Walker Barn to buy cigarettes. The quarry office was situated where the Tegg's Nose Country Park visitor centre and tea room are today. Some of the quarry workers lived at 'Windyway House' on the site.

The quarry owner paid a weekly visit. He would leave his car at the kennels then walk down and have a brief look round and chat to the workers. They also had regular visits from the blacksmith at Walker Barn quarry to sharpen the tools.

Setter Dog pub, which was unusually a sub post office with a post box set in the bar.

Above: Windyway and 'Tegsnose' quarry were owned by Joseph Wetton and Sons Ltd who also had quarries at Kerridge, Walker Barn and Rainow. When Joseph Wetton died in 1907, over 200 of his men took part in the funeral procession from Bollington to Rainow. Wettons closed in 1964 and Windyway's 200 ft-deep hole was later used as a refuse tip with rubble from a collapsed railway embankment and spoil from the Hurdsfield ICI works.

Below: Saddlers Way, an old packhorse route to Langley by the quarry, and where there used to be another small quarry until 1920.

Tegg's Nose

Records indicate there had been quarrying here since at least the fifteenth century. It had been operated by Macclesfield Corporation since the 16th century but by the 1870s Harry S Aspinall was working the quarry. Joseph Wetton had acquired it by 1883 as part of the biggest company in the area. It eventually closed in 1956 when it was in the ownership of Ashton and Holmes. There used to be a house on the site, lived in by the quarry foreman which existed until 1929. It was last occupied by John Rose and family by 1871 until about 1885. He also had a small holding there with two cows.

In the 1960s explosives tests took place here conducted by Manchester University. The impact of the explosives used to shape metal caused windows in Langley to be regularly blown out. The site was strewn with leftover metal and wires. During testing, they were connected to detonators which were activated by plungers in pill boxes. After the tests finished, people began to visit the site.

Brocklehurst-Whiston were the owners in 1971 and they put the 100-acre site up for sale for £2000. It was purchased by Cheshire County Council as a picnic area and a warden appointed with two assistant wardens the following year. The site has been cleared of rubble, and there are now information panels about quarry life and its geology. Additional quarrying machinery has been brought in, view points erected, and waymarked footpaths laid out.

Right: The spoil heaps to the north, made with left-over material from the stone dressing in the oldest part of the quarry, now covered in heather.

Below: The layers of gritstone and shale at the quarry face. The rock crusher in the foreground is from Beeston Quarry, Bollington and not as big as the original crusher at Tegg's Nose.

LANGLEY

Rose Cottage and Hole House c1910, at Hole House Lane by the overflow reservoir from Tegg's Nose and Bottoms Reservoirs.

In 1911, James Hambleton, a silk block printer and family lived at Rose Cottage. Hole House was the home of Samuel White, an estate labourer, his wife and daughter who was a silk tie maker.

The lane had been previously known as Bollin Head Lane and Bollin Lane. Bollin Head tape mill, to the west of the cottages, was built about 1830. Later the mill was used for chair-making before it was demolished in 1969.

Hole House was later renamed Rock Cottage.

The first Methodist Chapel, built in 1826, quickly deteriorated with dry rot, and suffered a ceiling collapse, thankfully while no-one was present. As well as a Sunday school, an elementary day school was held here.

After the chapel was demolished, services were held for a year in a storeroom above a shop known as Langley Stores. The new chapel opened in 1858 at a cost of £1350 from public donations. Singing in the services was accompanied on clarinet and horn as organs were not generally used at that time.

Further renovations were made in 1881 and an organ installed in 1884. It was registered in 1889 to conduct marriages. In 1905 the Chapel Trustees included William Whiston, owner of Langley Print Works and other local manufacturers. There are only four graves in the chapelyard. The land at the side of the chapel was known as 'Dunstan Meadow' until the Forest Drive residences were built there with the first residents moving in during April 1968.

Langley Methodist Chapel with Dunstan Meadow in the foreground. 31 Main Road on the right, was the birthplace in 1901 of distinguished wildlife artist Charles Tunnicliffe. The family later moved to Lane Ends Farm.

St Dunstan pub on Main Road, had its licence granted to Hugh Roberts in 1825 on condition that there was no betting, bull, badger, or bear baiting or cockfighting there. St Dunstan (924-988) was Archbishop of Canterbury, patron saint of bellringers and of the blind.

The building in the centre was once a smallholding. Following a fire in 1913 it re-opened as Mrs Hesford's Toffee Shop. In 1932 it became a stationer's with a visiting barber on Thursday evenings, then later a butcher's.

Hall Terrace opposite Langley Hall. Local historian Cyril Dawson is the tallest of the children.

This is thought to be a child's stone coffin, in a field near Coal Pit Lane. The field used to be part of Langley Hall Farm and the coffin possibly made from stone from the nearby Pyegreave quarry, which was also used for the building of St James' Church Sutton. The stone had been donated by Miss Mary Twemlow of Sandbach who owned the quarry. The 'coffin' had been used as a cattle trough.

Above: The premises of the old Riverside mill silk printing, dyeing and finishing works are in the centre. The first works were originally established about 1808. The River Bollin was diverted to form a moat on the site known as Doe Meadow.

The laundry built in 1906 is on the right, with Langley Hall in the background.

Hall Yard was for some time the home of the Langley Works Fire Brigade. They began in 1920 with the fire-engine 'Merryweather' which had red and gold livery and solid rubber tyres. It was tested for its suitability with a trial run uphill to Standing Stone.

Right: The old works have been renovated into the North Lights Factory. They house the Silk Gardens exhibition and Persian indoor gardens which trace the journey of silk from China to Macclesfield. Groups are welcome to visit by appointment. The old manager's house has been converted into holiday cottages.

The River Bollin from the public footpath near Langley Hall. The waters were once fished for trout but the effluent from the nearby mills made it heavily polluted. Now it is a much cleaner waterway.

The footpath, looking towards Birch Knoll, which leads to the Hollins range of hills between Langley and Macclesfield. The Knoll was known by locals as 'Noah's Hill' because it used to be owned by Noah Whiston.

SUTTON

The Church House Inn c1916. A section of a newspaper from 1777 was uncovered in the pub whilst it was being decorated in the 1940s. The inn used to have a stream running continuously over the floor in the cellar and out into a grid. It is said to have helped keep the beer cool. There was also a 30ft-deep well in the cellar which supplied a pump in the yard and was also used by nearby houses. The water features were re-routed some time after the 1950s.

St James Church vicarage was completed in 1849 for the vicar, Thomas Hughes. Later he was involved in a dispute with the church, because he kept the proceeds of graves fees in contravention of the conditions stipulated by Mrs Newbold the donor of the church land. He eventually agreed to pay back the money. William Stonehewer, Mrs Newbold's son who died in 1871, led the action against Hughes. His gravestone reads: 'He was one of five trustees who carried out the conditions of his mother's gift of land to this Church'. The old vicarage was sold in 2014 and the proceeds used to build a new one in the garden.

ERECTED A.D. 1845.
WILLIAM HULME
CHARLES CORBISHLEY
JAMES ROBINSON
JAMES SMITH

SURVEYORS
OF THE
TOWNSHIP
OF SUTTON

Stray animals were placed in the pinfold and released after the owner had paid a fine. It is one of only eight intact surviving examples in Cheshire, where there used to be over 150 pinfolds.

Left: Yew Tree Villa was previously the site of a thatched cottage built by John Warren, an apprentice of Robert Longden the wheelwright (see Plough House page 44). It was said that the old brick cottage been built on land that no-one owned and that John lived there rent and rate-free, and claimed the property as his own.

The small brick cottage, garden and orchard were purchased by Solomon Longden in an auction at the Old King's Head and he built Yew Tree Villa in 1877. He was listed there in 1891 as a retired builder and died two years later.

Former wheel-wright's shop at Gurnett by the River Bollin.

Top: The stone inscription indicates the house was built for Robert Longden and his wife Sarah in 1802. Longden used the building opposite for his wheelwright business.

Above: The house later became the Plough Inn (on the left-hand side of the photo). It is shown on an 1870s OS map as 'God Speed the Plough', meaning success in endeavours, which originated in an old ploughmans' song. This was traditionally sung on Plough Monday - the first Monday after Christmas when people returned to work.

The inn was also known by the shortened name of 'Speed the Plough'

in 1861 when Solomon Longden was the publican as well as stonemason.

In 1864 the Slack family were listed here as beer retailers. They had been farmers, and Ralph who was there in 1871 was also a paper manufacturer. His widow, Martha, born at Macclesfield Forest, continued to run the inn until she died in 1896, despite the attempts of the North Brewery Company to end her tenancy in 1891. In 1911 James Gouldstrap took over the tenancy of the 'Speed the Plough' from James Lomas, buying the fixtures and contents of the inn for nearly £17. By 1925 it had closed and became the home of William and Lavinia Etchells. Today it is known as Plough House.

James Lomas and his wife Mary.

Peter Jackson

44

The Old King's Head Inn is believed to date back to 1695. Joseph Wardle, the inn keeper from about 1819, was given a giant mushroom in 1834 picked in a field at Sutton Hall. It measured two feet five and a half inches in width. The Jackson family ran the pub from the 1870s for over three decades. In 1932, the landlady, Mrs JH Reed, won an Austin car for the best twenty word slogan for Kensitas cigarettes. She was successful on her fifteenth attempt, which coincided with her wedding anniversary. The old smithy next door to the inn is seen in the old photos.

The 108 steps are to be seen in the centre, to right of the Millstone inn yard.

MACCLESFIELD

108 Steps, Bunkers Hill and Step Hill all led down from Church Street to Waters Green, and Brunswick Street went down to Brunswick Hill. By 1841 they housed weavers and spinners. Today the 108 Steps, Step Hill and Brunswick Hill are still in use.

The origin of the 108 Steps is uncertain but it was presumably an ancient way from the old castle ramparts. This area of connecting routes was known as the Gutters and pulled down in 1907. It included an old dwelling at the top of the 108 Steps in the 'magpie' style which may either have been the old Macclesfield Grammar School or the home of the parish priest in pre-Reformation times.

The 108 Steps were constructed with kerbs and setts quarried from Tegg's Nose. It was a pedestrian route but users in the 1840s would have been shocked and amazed to see it regularly used by a man on horseback. This was John Clayton, a former Sergeant Major in the King's Dragoons for 34 years. After retiring from the regiment he joined the Cheshire Yeomanry but suffered a riding accident which caused his erratic behaviour on the Steps. The police told him to stop on each occasion and he was eventually brought to court over another offence. A local surgeon testified that Clayton was unfit to stand trial and the court ordered him to be taken back to his wife to be looked after.

Some locals remember a tunnel running from the garage yard of the Millstone Inn next to the the 108 Steps up to a cobbler's shop. It was said to be arched in Flemish brick with iron holders for torches and big enough for a horse and trap. The entrance to the tunnel collapsed and was filled with rubble.

David & Barbara Bullock

Right: David Bullock in the garage in the 1960s which led to the tunnel entrance. The garage belonged to his father-in-law who ran the cafe next door.

47

During the 16th century in Macclesfield, a large glove was hung outside the window of the old Town Hall during the Wakes Fair. Everyone was free from arrest within the township while going to and from the Fair. This exemption from prosecution was taken advantage of by local villains.

The River Bollin was culverted at Waters Green with the building of Central Station in 1873.

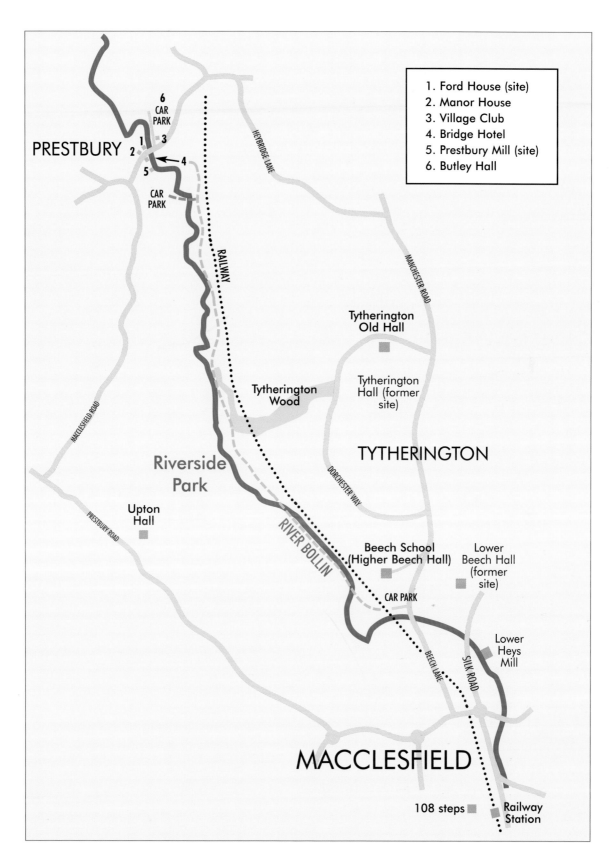

PRESTBURY

6
CAR
PARK

1
3
2
4
5

CAR
PARK

1. Ford House (site)
2. Manor House
3. Village Club
4. Bridge Hotel
5. Prestbury Mill (site)
6. Butley Hall

HEYBRIDGE LANE

RAILWAY

MANCHESTER ROAD

Tytherington
Old Hall

Tytherington
Wood

Tytherington
Hall (former
site)

TYTHERINGTON

MACCLESFIELD ROAD

Riverside
Park

DORCHESTER WAY

PRESTBURY ROAD

Upton
Hall

RIVER BOLLIN

Beech School
(Higher Beech Hall)

Lower
Beech Hall
(former
site)

CAR PARK

BEECH LANE

SILK ROAD

Lower
Heys
Mill

MACCLESFIELD

108 steps

Railway
Station

South front of Tytherington House.

TYTHERINGTON

Tytherington Hall stood on land now known as Hall Close and Hall Grove. In 1813 it was part of the 'Titherington House Estate' which was purchased in 1812 by William Brocklehurst, a solicitor and banker who also had a country seat at Swythamley Hall near Leek. At his death in 1859 he bequeathed it to his two brothers, but his adopted nephew Philip Brocklehurst, a silk manufacturer, continued to live at Tytherington and at Swythamley.

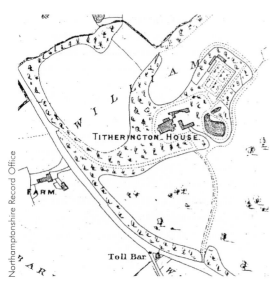

Philip was made a baronet the year before his death in 1904, and was Deputy Lieutenant of Staffordshire, and a JP. He was keen on country sports and described as 'blunt but genial'. He requested that when he died, his coffin should be carried by workmen who had been longest in his employment.

His eldest son, Sir Philip Lee Brocklehurst, at the age of twenty one, accompanied Ernest Shackleton on the two-year British Antarctic expedition which started out in 1907. He was ill-equipped and inexperienced for such hazardous conditions and had to have a toe removed because of frostbite. Later he was awarded the medal of the Royal Geographical Society for his part in the record-breaking achievement. Sir Philip kept the frost-bitten toe in a jar at Swythamley Hall. During World War I he served with the 1st Life Guards and later made a journey of over 5000 miles across Africa in a Chevrolet car.

The hall at Tytherington was rebuilt in 1870 at a cost of over £50,000 by Ann the wife of William Coare Brocklehurst who had inherited the estate. She had done it as a surprise for her spouse while he was away in London serving as the MP for Macclesfield. However, William was said to have been unimpressed with his first sight of the newly-completed mansion, and refused to see any more of it. They reputedly never lived there, preferring Butley Hall, Prestbury.

For the next decade, Tytherington Hall was unoccupied, then Henry Charlton, a finisher of cotton goods in Manchester, came to live there in 1883. The impressive hall and gardens required a staff of fifteen. Charlton was a Cheshire magistrate for many years and, at the time of his death in 1915, one of the oldest members of the Prestbury Division Bench. He was also Deputy Chairman of the Board at St Mary's Hospital Manchester. Charlton was noted for his philanthropic works and each Christmas all the children in Tytherington received a gift from him, delivered in wheelbarrows by his gardeners.

In 1897 all the children of Tytherington and their parents were invited to the hall in celebration of the Queen's Diamond Jubilee for a meal and games, and to explore the grounds. The fun continued until dusk when the National Anthem was played and everyone was served sandwiches, lemonade and milk. Amongst the beneficiaries in Charlton's will were St Mary's Hospital and Dispensary, and refuges for boys and girls at Strangeways, Manchester.

The Marlborough College for girls was next to occupy the hall in 1919. The private college had been established by Miss Anna Ashmall Salt at Marlborough Road, Buxton in 1893 before moving to Tytherington. The Buxton college site was described as the 'finest climate in England for delicate and growing girls'. Miss Salt was the daughter of a Staffordshire solicitor and had previously been head of Hope Lea girls' boarding school at Heaton Norris until 1891, when she left to work on a patent for an improved dress suspender.

The college at Tytherington was advertised in 1919 as being set in 70 acres of parkland at an altitude of 500 ft. The mansion was 'modern' and a 'sound education' given with 'individual attention'. There

Buxton Museum

Miss Anna Ashmall Salt and the Marlborough College pupils.

was a Domestic Economy Department, and special training for entrance into the Faculty of Medicine.

Miss Salt was also a supporter of a new building extension for a sick animals' dispensary at Pendleton, Salford donating fittings and equipment in 1927. While Principal of the Buxton college she founded a free convalescent home for poor Manchester and Salford children. Anna, who was also an accomplished pianist, died following a five week illness in 1930.

By the time of the Second World War, the college had closed and the hall was used for military training. Ken Adams, a medical orderly in the Royal Medical Corps, was transferred to Tytherington Hall in 1941. He described it as a dirty place with inadequate toilet facilities, where he attended lectures on nursing and dealing with the effects of explosives. During 1942 the Cheshire Home Guard held training camps here in preparation for possible enemy invasion.

Nissen huts were erected in the grounds for American troops who came during preparations for the D-Day landing in Normandy. The 825th Tank Destroyer Battalion arrived there on the 7th June 1944 but because of the limited facilities, one of three companies had to be stationed at a school hall in Macclesfield.

The troops were given instruction in British radio procedure, and translating messages into code. Soldiers soon made friends in Macclesfield and the phrase 'Any gum chum' quickly caught on around the camp. As a mark of respect, three members of the Battalion were invited to attend a meeting of Macclesfield Council. Five weeks later the Battalion, code-named 'Highway', made their way south. The US 133rd Anti-Aircraft Military Gun Battalion were billeted at the the Hall in September 1944.

Below, and opposite page: Photographs from the College prospectus.

Molly Spink

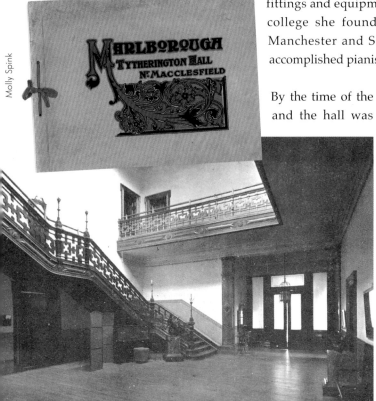

College entrance hall.

Gls at Tytherington

Drive to the College

The Hall became derelict after the War, and in 1945 the company administrating the estate went into liquidation. A plan of the 'Tytherington Park Estate' was submitted in 1954 for planning permission showing the division of land for housing. It was announced in April 1957 that Jack Broadhead, a local garage owner and sports car racing enthusiast, had purchased the site in order to demolish the Hall and build twelve houses. The Wimpey company also announced they were to build homes. A bungalow at Hall Close suffered subsidence which was thought to have been caused by the old Hall site.

Lake in the College grounds.

Main College entrance.

The Hall today.

Tytherington Study Group

The Hall before restoration in 1984

Tytherington Old Hall

This was once the residence of the Worth family who had held the manor of Tytherington for three centuries after it passed into the ownership of Robert de Worth from the de Tyderington family c1398. Many of the Worths are buried in the St Nicholas family chapel at Prestbury Church.

The Old Hall was mentioned in the 1581 will of Philip Worth who bequeathed to his son his clock and all the glass, along with the looking-glass in the parlour, and ten shillings to each of the servants in his employment. Records show Jasper Worth was taken to Prestbury Church at the age of seven in 1599 to marry Penelope, aged only five, the daughter of Sir William Davenport of Bramhall Hall. The last of the Worths, Jasper, died in 1693 and his estates passed to his cousin Samuel Heath of Dublin. By the 1830's they were owned by Sir Edward Stracey and the Hall occupied by Joseph Lockett, a farmer.

The land was being farmed in 1841 by Thomas Mayson, followed by Joseph Lockett again about 1851. Part of the Old Hall estate was purchased by Thomas Brocklehurst of the Fence near Macclesfield in 1855, and it passed through the family to Peter Pownall Brocklehurst. It is thought that alterations were made to the Hall around the 1860s including a stone property built onto the Old Hall.

Between about 1857 and the 1870s Bancroft Pierpoint Cook farmed the 232-acre estate. Then Samuel Redway occupied the hall in 1881 and he was succeeded by Henry Wallworth JP by 1888. He patented and sold a potato sorter and by 1912 was the chairman of both Macclesfield Rural District Council and House Committee. After his death in 1924 the farm passed to his son Percy, who had retired to live at Lower Beech Hall by 1939 and died in 1958.

In 1988 work began to restore the abandoned Old Hall at a cost of £100,000, as part of a new housing development. It was intended to open it as a meeting place and provide social facilities for retired people in the nearby mews housing. The farmhouse which had been built onto the hall, causing subsidence and cracking to the old building, was demolished. Kerridge stone slates from an old farm being demolished at Wincle were used in the roof restoration, and the timber for the replacement gable was from the Royal Sandringham estate. The Hall has now been converted into a private residence.

The Old Hall c1950.

The farmhouse prior to demolition

Macclesfield Mueums

The Hall today.

The Hall 1855.

55

Higher Beech Hall

Today it is Beech Hall School, established in 1926, but the estate had been in the ownership of the Worth family who held the manor of Tytherington from the time of Edward I until 1695 and was known in the 17th century as 'Bache Hall'. John Worth was the last in the family line. He died without a successor in 1669, and the estate passed to a cousin in Dublin. The estate went through a series of owners before it was inherited by William Brooksbank in 1769. In 1832 it passed to Sir Edward Stracey Bart after marrying William's daughter Anne. 'Higher Beech' had also been the residence of John Parker Mosley in 1779 when he became Lord of the Manor in Manchester.

Northamptonshire Record Office

Illustration from the 1855 catalogue.

Edward, after his father's death in 1829, succeeded to the baronetcy and moved to the family seat at Rackheath Hall, Norfolk. He was a magistrate in Cheshire as well as Norfolk and Suffolk. Born in India and educated at Oxford he became Clerk to the House of Commons. He was a close friend of the Earl of Shaftesbury for whom he was a legal advisor.

There was a fatal stabbing close to the gates of 'Beach Hall' in 1822. John Brooks was returning to his home at the Blue Bell inn from Macclesfield one evening when he was attacked and killed by a passing stranger. In 1825, one of Stacey's bee hives at the 'Beach' produced an extraordinary quantity of over 85lbs of honey. When Stracey died at Rackheath Hall in 1851, his coffin was carried, at his request, by twenty of his estate workers who were each given a black suit.

Major Joseph Brooksbank rented 'The Beach' from his cousin, Lady Stracey, until he inherited the Stracey estate. He served with the 24th Foot Regiment and 26th Cameronians and was a county magistrate until he died in 1853.

Major Brooksbank had no successors and the Higher Beach, Lower Beach and the Old Hall estates were put up for sale in 1855, with the former being purchased by Thomas Wardle about 1857. He had been

VALUABLE MANSIONS, PARKS, FARMS, VILLA SITES, ACCOMMODATION LANDS, HOUSES, AND PREMISES.
(COMPRISING UPWARDS OF 700 ACRES,)
IN AND NEAR
MACCLESFIELD, TITHERINGTON, HURDSFIELD, AND PRESTBURY,
IN THE COUNTY OF CHESTER.

Macclesfield Courier

1855 catalogue

Sir Philip Lancaster Brocklehurst

Section of the Wardle stained glass window at Beech Hall School

Mayor of Macclesfield in 1839 and had many roles as Councillor and Alderman between 1837 and 1850. He and his brother Henry had a silk-manufacturing business in the town, and when he died in 1868 virtually the whole of Macclesfield closed for his funeral procession. The local newspaper said he was one of the town's oldest and most deeply respected residents.

During his time at the Beach, Wardle had made additions and improvements to the property, and the sale notices described it as a first-class family mansion in every way. Stewart Gladstone, an East India merchant, lived there with his family until about 1876. By 1881 landowner and magistrate Philip Lancaster Brocklehurst was in residence with his three domestic servants. He also owned Swythamley Hall in Staffordshire, where he spent more of his time. The Hall then seems to have been generally unoccupied for almost twenty years.

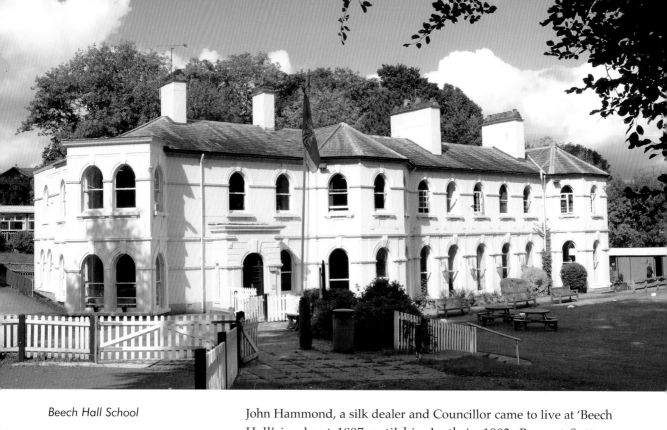

Beech Hall School

Edwin Crew JP

John Hammond, a silk dealer and Councillor came to live at 'Beech Hall' in about 1897 until his death in 1902. Born at Sutton, he was an apprentice in his uncle's silk business before forming his own companies at Park Green, Macclesfield and Leek. Although he served on many committees he rarely spoke at Council, but was genial, kind-hearted and popular throughout the town. He was a director of the Cheshire Building Society, and committee member of the Macclesfield Useful Knowledge Society, an organisation to improve education, which originated at the Roe Street Sunday School Macclesfield. The Society's former offices on Park Green are within the premises of Weatherspoons and known as 'The Society Rooms'. They also housed the first girls high school in Macclesfield.

Beech Hall was advertised to let in 1905 as 'a very desirable residence with fine views, good gardens and stabling'. Edwin Crew, a former silk manufacturer and Mayor of Macclesfield lived there from 1909 until 1911, followed by William Hampson, a cloth finisher, for the next four years. In about 1910 the Hall had been split into two homes with a second drive providing separate access. The 1911 Census also listed John Thomas Lomas, a retired Manchester manufacturer who remained there until 1915. Edwin Crew returned to Higher Beech from 1918 until October 1924 when the Hall was again for sale.

It was bought by Mr and Mrs Wilfred Edwards to re-open as a boys' preparatory school, which began advertising for pupils between the ages of six and fourteen the following February. The school was 'set in many acres of grounds amidst the sunny Cheshire hills...with large airy classrooms and dormitories... and food and health entirely in the hands of the headmaster's wife'. Wilfred Edwards went into retirement in Buckinghamshire and the school was taken over in 1935 by John Hunt and his wife Evelyn, who increased numbers from thirty-five to 128. Hugh Worthington joined the staff in 1952. He married Penelope, the headmaster's daughter, and became head in 1970. The school became co-educational in 1981, and now has 180 pupils and a nursery.

Replica of the burial urn found at Beech Hall School

The Hall stands on the site of a Bronze Age defensive settlement, and during excavation for the construction of a school swimming pool in 1960, a builder thought he had struck an old drain two feet below the surface. It was later identified as a burial urn containing the bones of a woman about twenty years old. The bones had been incinerated and pounded into fragments to place into the collared urn. The school site is thought to be situated on a former burial ground containing many more urns. The Tytherington urn is now at the Grosvenor Museum, Chester.

A burial mound known locally as 'Tellytubby Hill' with charred bones from the same period, was later discovered at a housing estate to the north of the school. The site had been disturbed by the Home Guard during WWII whilst digging trenches for a gun emplacement, but investigation of their spoil heap revealed the fragments of an urn and bones. A Bronze Age perforated limestone hammer has been found in a field near Tytherington Hall. Evidence of an ancient lake was discovered during construction of the railway through Tytherington, along with the remains of a red deer antler and an oak paddle.

In the 1990s, housing developers wanted to convert part of the Hall into five luxury flats and demolish the rest. The school found it difficult to find alternative premises and eventually came to an agreement with the developers in 2002 to remain at the Hall.

Beech Hall School

Lower Beech Hall

The Hall was situated opposite the present Lower Beech Farm behind Tytherington School, and once part of the estate inherited by the Stracey family from the Brooksbanks in 1832.

Lower Beech Hall

Mill owner Charles Wood lived there from 1806 until 1817. In 1812 there were disturbances in the neighbourhood and a mob attacked the house. From 1818 it had been the home of Richard Wood who owned the old Mill Lane cotton mill in Macclesfield with his brother Charles. He was an Alderman, and two of his brothers had been Mayors of the town.

Wood moved to 'Westbrook', Macclesfield in 1833 and Lower Beech was advertised to let. It was described as a 'capital mansion fit for a gentleman with a large family' and 'beautifully situated near to the turnpike road from London to Manchester'. Lower Beech was then occupied by Nathaniel Pearson until his death in 1842. Pearson and his brother James owned a substantial five-storey silk mill on Chester Road in Macclesfield.

Samuel Bayley, who took over Lower Heyes Cotton Mill on the banks of the River Bollin in 1843, moved into Lower Beech in about 1847. In 1851 he employed over ninety people at the works site but later got into financial difficulties and was made bankrupt in 1856. When the ten-bedroomed Hall and 54 acres of land were advertised for sale in 1855, Bayley had already moved out. Bayley's mill and contents were for sale in March 1858. This comprised two four-storey and one three-storey mills, two houses, twenty-three cottages, counting house, smithy, warehouse and mechanic's shop. Samuel Bayley held a meeting with his creditors in 1861 and died in 1866 aged 67 at his home on Prestbury Road, Macclesfield.

The Higher and Lower Beech estates were purchased by Thomas Wardle (see Higher Beech Hall), and the former became the home of Thomas Oldham and family in about 1860. He was born in Cork, Ireland and listed on the 1861 census as a house and land proprietor. Seven years later he and his family moved out of the nine-bedroomed house and auctioned it off along with furniture, paintings and sculpture.

In about 1875, Edward Eaton JP and manufacturer of dye ingredients at Fountain Street, Macclesfield, moved into Lower Beech Hall. He allowed his home to be used for a Royal Commission enquiry into whether the two local MPs had used bribes to gather votes. The 1881 report confirmed that corruption had taken place and the town became part of the East Cheshire constituency. After Eaton's death here in 1888, Milner Gibson who had a calico printing business on Portland Street, Manchester moved in with his family and servants. By then the property included ten bedrooms, two greenhouses, stabling and a large garden set within six acres of land.

Hercules Yates JP

Gibson moved to Hazel Grove by about 1903, and Lower Beech Hall was occupied by Hercules Campbell Yates in 1910. He was the son of a judge, and became one of the best-known people in public office in Cheshire. For fifty years he was Coroner for East Cheshire, Registrar and High Bailiff to Macclesfield County Court for forty-seven years, and a long-serving magistrate for the Prestbury area. He was also chairman of the Cheshire Quarter Sessions as well as a member of Macclesfield Board of Guardians for thirty-two years. In addition he was Honorary Major of the 5th Volunteer Battalion of the Cheshire Regiment. He died in 1931 aged 80 at Lower Beech Hall.

By 1933 Lower Beech Hall was being advertised as part of the Hurdsfield Estate, which included Upton Hall and twenty dairy farms in an area of about 1272 acres of building land. In 1939 it was the home of retired farmer Percy Wallworth, formerly of Tytherington Old Hall, along with bank clerk Ronald Sheldon and his wife Maude.

In 1961 the 'commodious Georgian residence' together with nearly five acres were being offered as a residential development. On the 1987 OS map the Hall had been demolished to make way for new housing, although the old farm building and adjoining cottages remained.

Northamptonshire Record Office

The toll bar house Beech Lane, Tytherington c1914.

Upton Hall

James Croston (1830-1893), a Manchester magistrate and manufacturer, came to live here in 1874. He held many offices including Conservative Councillor for Cheetham, Secretary of the Northern Church Defence Association and leader of the Lancashire Constitutional Association, and was active on the Manchester School Board. When many cotton workers became destitute owing to the American Civil War, he was part of a committee which helped to organise relief.

But he was also noted for his work in the antiquarian field. Amongst his many books were the highly popular 'On Foot Through the Peak' (1860), and 'Nooks and Corners of Lancashire and Cheshire' He also edited a new edition of the 'History of the County Palatine and Duchy of Lancaster'. He was the historian of the prestigious 'John Shaw's Club' in Manchester and also found time to campaign for free and compulsory education.

His full and productive life came to an end one evening when he died suddenly while travelling home from Manchester by train to Prestbury. He had been a tireless worker in politics and the church, a gifted speaker and dedicated historian, and his death provoked much sadness among his many friends.

Opposite: Blue Bell Valley Tytherington c1902. Blue Bell Lane still exists, and there used to be a Blue Bell Inn and Blue Bell Farm in the district.

PRESTBURY

The Bridge hotel by the river Bollin.

Bridge Hotel

This was once a farmhouse built in 1626. The tithe map c1838 indicates it was owned by the Legh family and occupied by Martha Goodwin. The Thompstone family, who worked the corn mill behind the church, lived here from about 1851 to 1883.

By 1939 it had become an eight-bed-roomed hotel with a cafe seating fifty, managed by Edwin Stiles and his wife. In 1953, despite local opposition from the people in the properties opposite, Frances Joseph Whiteside was granted a licence for dancing and music with a three-piece band of violin, piano and cello. The dance space was 8ft square, and the dancing was limited to those having meals.

In 1955 Whiteside was granted a full licence despite opposition from the District Licensed Victuallers' Association, on condition that consumption of alcohol only took place with meals costing no less than 3s 6d per head. Whitehead said his hotel had served 55,000 main meals and the lowest price charged was 13s 6d. The Whitesides were still in ownership in 1961 and the following year it was Egon Ronay-recommended with three stars in the new guide.

The Bridge Hotel previously had an entrance onto the road.

Bridge Hotel restaurant c 1953

Ford House

The hall probably dates back to the 17th century, and by the 1840s it was owned by the Legh family and was the premises of the Roe Buck public house occupied by James Crowder. The house had been rebuilt sometime in the mid-nineteenth century.

It had become the home of retired surgeon Thomas Goodier Richmond in about 1867. He studied at Manchester School of Medicine, then Guy's and St Thomas's hospitals in London. He had surgeries at Gartside Street and Coburg Terrace in Manchester, then moved to Hulme where he witnessed the terrible insanitary

Ford house had long been a familiar landmark at the end of the street.

conditions in the district during a cholera and other epidemics between 1849 and 1852. Through his improvements, the severity of later outbreaks was lessened. He realised that public health was affected by local conditions and campaigned for twenty years to have the Bridgewater Canal cleansed, as it was regarded at the time as an open sewer.

At his death in 1887, he was described as 'a man of unobtrusive habit, kindly disposition, and courtly manners, and though in the course of a long life he made many friends, he never lost the respect of one'. Dr Richmond donated the costs for a number of windows at St Peter's Church, opposite his house, where he was a warden.

He left £1000 in his will to his old school, Manchester Grammar, to found the Richmond Scholarship which funded a scholar for three years with preference given to poor students.

Mrs Annie Handford, the widow of a tea dealer, together with her family, were at the house by 1890 and remained there until her death in 1923. The house at that time had four bedrooms, a three-stall stable, coachhouse and harness-room and greenhouses. Between 1924-1929 it was the home of John and Alice Lawton, then from 1930 to 1947, George Price and son, bread and cake manufacturers in Manchester, lived there. Herbert Hope, who had a fish and chip business at Bramhall, died there in 1951.

By 1969 it was in use as parish church offices and community centre until it was forced to close in 2007 due to its poor condition. The church had hoped to redevelop the site but owing to difficulties with the planning authorities decided to sell the site in 2013 for a residential development and the house has been demolished.

Above: Ford House now the site of a new housing development.

Below: The house prior to demolition.

The Manor House

It is thought to have been the site of the cells of the Monks of St Werburgh and the garden still contains the medicinal herbs they would have used. In 1696 the 'vicaridge house' contained seven 'bayes cowe houses and hay houses', then in 1708 it was rebuilt and remained the vicarage until 1891 when Canon Reginald Broughton moved to a new home.

St Peter's Church c1940.

By 1906 it was the home of Albert Lees, a director of Lees Brothers, cotton spinners at the Albert Mills, Hollinwood, Oldham. Born in Oldham, he was a major in the Territorial Army, and married to Elizabeth Bibby, the daughter of a Liverpool ship owner. He had left Prestbury with his family by 1916 to live at Rowton Castle near Shrewsbury and was also on the board of the Lancashire and Yorkshire Railway Company.

Between 1922 and 1929, William Taylor Birchenough JP who was previously at Gawsworth Hall, lived here. He was married to Jane Peacock, the daughter of Richard, a founder of the locomotive manufacturer Beyer-Peacock. William was a director of the family business John Birchenough and Sons silk mills at Park Lane and Wardle Street Macclesfield. They specialised in contracts for Government departments, presumably helped by brother, Henry, being on various Government committees.

The house used to draw its water supply through this hand pump.

Flooring from the previous house built in 1708.

Conditions at the mills were commended by visiting American women's rights activist, Emily Faithful, who said that the women looked more healthy than those in the Manchester factories. She was also impressed with all the decorations in the mills celebrating the marriage of the owner's son, which showed there was a good relationship between the management and workers. The business was later sold and it then traded under the name of Josiah Smale and Son Ltd.

The Birchenough family was involved with various charities in the town including the Technical and Art Schools and William's grandfather had been mayor in 1876. William's son was a member of the Harrow Public School cricket team which was involved in a memorable two-day match with Eton College in 1910. It was known as 'Fowler's Match' following the outstanding performance of the Eton captain Robert St Leger Fowler who was top scorer and took twelve wickets. By the time of William's death in 1932 he was at Prestbury Hall with his daughter Mrs Armitage. His friend Col Brocklehurst said that William, both in business and pleasure, was respected and loved, and a gentleman of the highest character.

By 1939 William Jewison, a dental surgeon, born in Withington Manchester, the son of a sugar broker, lived here. Within living memory, locals remember coming for treatment here. The current owners removed frosted glass from the old waiting room.

Spencer Brook flows through the garden before entering the river Bollin.

Above: The Black Boy was a 16th century inn where Bonnie Prince Charlie is reputed to have stayed on his march to Derby. It is said to have got its name through a misunderstanding over its previous name of the Saracen's Head when a travelling artist wrongly painted the black boy on the sign. Today it is known as the Legh Arms after the area's land owners, but the inn sign shows both names.

The old mill c1908.

Prestbury Mill

The mill at Prestbury was known as Hamlyn's Mill following the company's takeover from Wrights in 1946. Hamlyn and Co was founded in 1859 by Peter Lesoufe in London and expanded with branches throughout the country. They specialised in producing animal foodstuffs and supplying yeast and barley to Scottish distillers. The provender plant at Prestbury employed twenty-nine in 1959 and supplied their products to five counties. The joint managers of the plant, Mr L Heywood and Mr AE Lomas had served 36 and 28 years with the company respectively.

Above: The new extension to the mill following the 1940 fire.

Opposite: The old mill, and the now demolished footbridge.

A fire in 1940 did not totally destroy the old mill building, and part of it was incorporated into the new three-storey building. A 1678 datestone, although cracked by the heat from the fire, was rescued from the brickwork. The surviving stone structure was thought to have been earlier than the old mill and used by monks for grinding corn and weaving.

The fire broke out while the foreman miller was responding to a phone call which he was unable to understand, and never established who it was. It was believed that the fire had burned through the mill so quickly because it had been drawn under the premises through a water channel.

By 1951, only part of the original buildings remained on the site, including the old cottage in the yard and stables. In place of the old mill, there was now a modern corn mill.

The mill cottage by the Bollin.

Collar House, now the Beaumont Care Home, Collar House Drive

Prestbury Village Club

Portrait of Isaac Crewdson Waterhouse which hangs in the Village Club.

Isaac Crewdson Waterhouse lived at Collar House, Prestbury, for twenty-six years. He was a generous donor to local and religious causes and provided Prestbury with the Village Club as an alternative venue to pubs. Crewdson was a member of the temperance movement and his grandfather the founder of the Manchester City Mission.

At his sudden death in 1913, it was said that 'it was impossible to think what the village would be like without Mr Waterhouse, every man woman and child would feel they had lost a real friend'. The Institute closed for a week and a muffled peal of bells rang at his funeral.

74

One Prestbury local who was born in 1899 recalled how the village policeman used to stand in the road with his hands on his hips just to let people know he was there. He was friendly and helpful but if any of the local boys got into mischief he would lock them in his cellar for about an hour to remind them to behave properly.

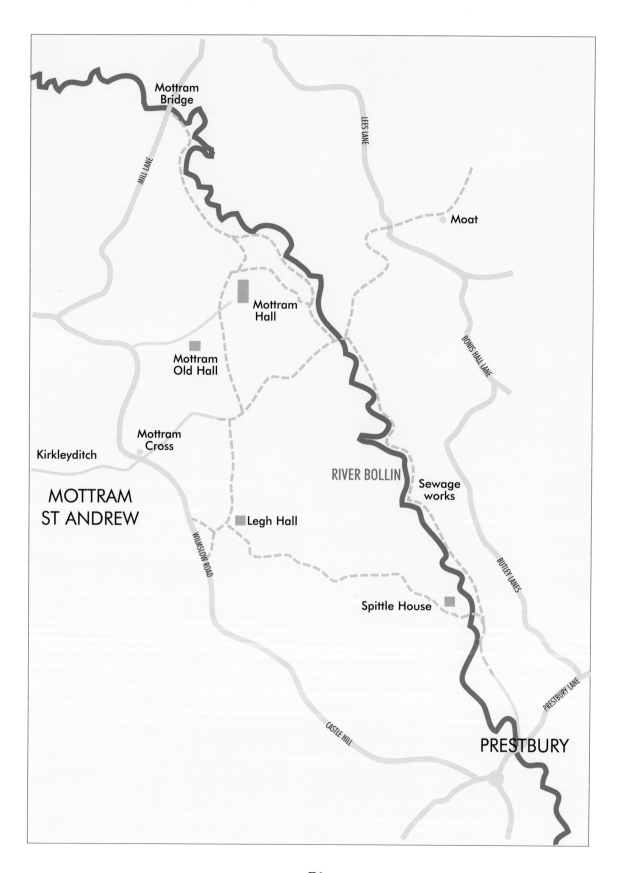

Mottram
Bridge

MILL LANE

LEES LANE

Moat

Mottram
Hall

BONIS HALL LANE

Mottram
Old Hall

Mottram
Cross

Kirkleyditch

RIVER BOLLIN

Sewage
works

MOTTRAM
ST ANDREW

Legh Hall

WILMSLOW ROAD

BUTLEY LANES

Spittle House

CASTLE HILL

PRESTBURY LANE

PRESTBURY

Mottram cross in its previous position alongside the road.

Mottramite

The peaceful village of Kirkleyditch, Mottram St Andrew, was the scene of an amazing discovery when it was claimed that a new mineral, vanadium, had been found here. Vanadium was used in the production of steel. Chemist Sir Henry Enfield Roscoe informed the Royal Society in 1876 that it had been discovered in ore piles waiting to be treated at the mine and had been named Mottramite. The mine had been worked by various companies for seven years up to 1867.

But in 1954 various experts decided the piles had been transported from Pim Hill in Shropshire where vanadium had been mined between 1875 and 1876. However, Byron Carroll Weege, an American expert and collector of minerals, who was living at Mottram St Andrew in 1980 was told by a local woodcutter that in certain weather conditions he could hear a 'bagpipe sound' in his garden.

The site was investigated and two huge sandstone slabs were located which capped a brick-lined shaft. This went down twenty feet, followed by about fifteen feet of hand-cut sandstone. From here levels led off in two directions and various samples of mineral were brought back up. This was later confirmed as a form of Mottramite, and after further exploration of the seam and analysis involving staff at the British Museum it was identified as 'vanadian duftite'.

No further work was done on the site, the mine has flooded and is now inaccessible. The cottages on the property have been replaced by a new residence.

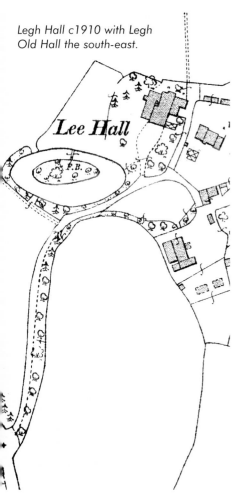

Legh Hall c1910 with Legh Old Hall the south-east.

Legh Hall

Known as Lee Hall when it was built in the 1850s to replace the old hall, and by 1861 it was the home of James Street, a captain in the Royal Artillery, and his wife Julia. They assumed the surname of Wright by Royal licence in 1885, and James died in 1889.

Henry Morgan was next to live at the hall by about 1870. He was listed as a farmer of 60 acres and also a former railway secretary of several lines including the Birmingham, Wolverhampton and Stour Valley, the northern section of the London and North Western, and the Oldham and Guide Bridge Railway. Bradshaw's 1845 guide lists him as a director of the Bristol and Exeter Railway company. He was also a strong campaigner within the temperance movement. His wife Hannah had a 'colourful' grandfather who got married in an orange-coloured suit and was the first person in Bristol to carry an umbrella. By 1882 an extension had been built onto the hall which became the home of the estate gardener.

Solicitor Walter Greg and family were at the Hall by 1890. He was the grandson of Samuel the founder of Styal Mill, and was head of the firm of Cunliffe and Greg, solicitors in Manchester, and had been Under Sheriff for Cheshire and Lancashire. He played international football and had helped to introduce lacrosse to the Manchester area. Locally, he was manager of Mottram School and chairman of the Parish Council.

78

His wife, Susan, was the cousin of novelist Elizabeth Gaskell. Her father, Robert Gaskell, originally lived in Warrington where he was a councillor and secretary of the local Anti-Slavery Society and a supporter of equal rights for women. Susan Greg was known not only for the many ways in which she helped and supported the people of the village, but also as a prominent campaigner for women's and children's rights. She was President of the North of England Society for Women's Suffrage, and Treasurer of the Wage Earning Children's Committee who spoke out against the 'Half-Time' system, which required children to work in the morning and then be educated in the afternoon. In meetings around the country she argued that it was difficult for the 'little white slaves' to learn anything following an early start at the factory or mill.

She was known as 'Macclesfield's Lady Bountiful' because there was hardly a charity in the district with which she was not connected. Most notable of these were the Macclesfield Public Health Society and the Macclesfield School for Mothers which she continually supported.

Walter Greg died while in Egypt in 1906, but his wife Susan continued to live at the hall with her daughter Margaret until her death in 1932. Willy De Cort, a Belgian war refugee, whom she befriended as a boy, was present at her funeral service. He was a student at the Royal College of Music and he played her favourite piece of music, Bach's 'Air on a G String' on the violin as the coffin was brought into church. Their daughter Elizabeth married her cousin Walter Greg, who was knighted for his services to literature.

Walter Greg

Legh Hall from the north.

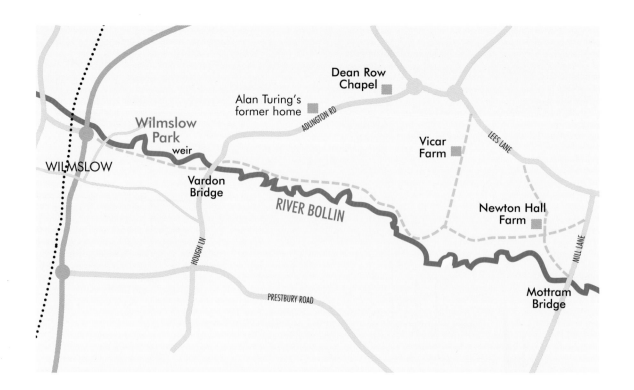

Newton Hall Farm

It was once one of the biggest farms in Cheshire and used to host the annual Adlington estate ploughing match. In 1892 the farm buildings were destroyed by a fire thought to have been started by a tramp. The farm hit the national headlines when a man was found dead in one of the farm lofts in 1959. The dead man, William Waters, had lived in the loft for forty years and was well-known in the area. He used to rise at 11.30am and collect blackberries and mushrooms which he sold in Wilmslow. Waters, born in Morley Wilmslow in 1887, worked as a waggoner in 1911 for a farmer in Woodford and had worked over the years as a general labourer; he had eaten at transport cafes or been fed by the locals. Jack Logan, an Irishman, also lived in the lofts and worked at nearby farms.

Converted farm buildings at Newton Hall Farm

After Walters had not been seen for three weeks, his body was found by farmer Frank Jackson, who noticed a 'funny smell' in the stable. Jackson found him lying in a sleeping position on a pile of old clothes. Around him were forty old coats and sacks, hundreds of empty cigarette packets and matchboxes, newspapers and a stack of old clothes. Beside him there was his pension book, and a watch on a brass chain in his cap. At the inquest, the coroner said that death was probably due to natural causes.

Newton Hall farm

Mottram Bridge had to be rebuilt at a cost of £1500 in 1872 following floods along the River Bollin. The swollen river in June of that year caused the drowning of a mother and child near Langley Hall, and the Hurdsfield Reservoir at Macclesfield to burst its banks. A forty-yard length of the Macclesfield Canal at Bollington gave way, which caused further devastation along the whole of the Bollin Valley.

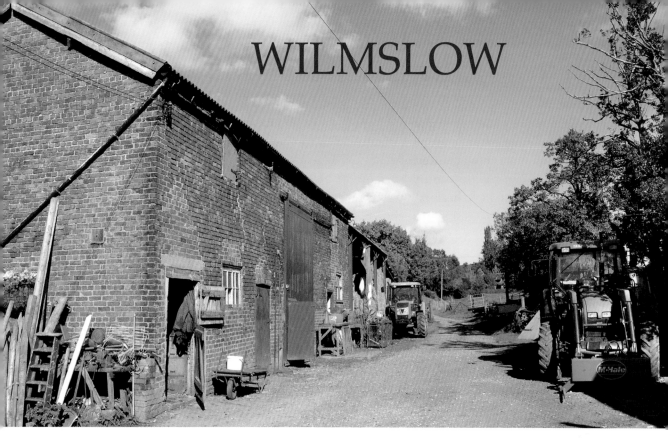

Vicar Farm

Top: Vicar Farm
Above: Phil Daniels and Mark Addy during filming of the BBC comedy series at the farm which is just off Lees Lane at Dean Row.

This is one of the few remaining working farms in the area, with beef and sheep farmed on the 42-acre estate. It was bought by brothers Harold and Joe Kelsall in 1921 for £2000, and continues to be owned by the Kelsall family.

The farm featured in the 1997 BBC TV comedy series 'Sunnyside Farm' which starred Mark Addy and Phil Daniels. The location manager had visited 100 farms before he came across the right one. He wanted a remote-looking farm which was not too difficult to reach. There were many slapstick scenes in the series made by Granada, and they even had to import extra supplies of mud (chocolate cake mix). One scene involved six cows getting on and off a specially reinforced coach with the seats taken out.

The present farmer, Phil Kelsall, said the programme makers 'roughed up' the farm to make it look uncared for, while he continued running the farm. This was Londoner Phil Daniels's first experience of a farm. Mark Addy had the frightening task of walking a bull around the farmyard, and was advised by the farmer that if the bull wants to go his own way, let him! The farm was also used in a tv production starring Rod Hull and Emu.

Dean Row Chapel

The Meeting House at Dean Row was completed in about 1694 and is thought to be one of the oldest places of Nonconformist worship in the area. Before its building, people had gathered at the home of John Worthington which was a licensed place of worship in 1689. Although the chapel could only hold about 200, it had a congregation of over 1300 'hearers' who came from all sections of society. It began as a Presbyterian church, but by 1848 it had departed from the traditional teachings and tenets of Christianity to become Unitarian.

By 1844 the chapel had become unfit for use, with cracked walls and broken windows. The congregation had dwindled and there was a possibility of another denomination gaining possession of the building. The minister, John Morris, would often be preaching just to his dog in order to receive his stipend (see page 86). After Morris's death, an appeal for funds was made and £300 of repairs and improvements were carried out in 1845. The pulpit was moved from the long north wall to the east end, the pews re-arranged, and the facing gallery removed. Also, rooms were built at the east end for use as a Sunday school and a day school. In 1862 a separate school was opened on Dean Row Road. After the school's closure in 1961 it became the Chapel hall.

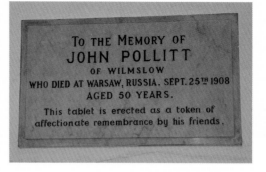

Memorial to John Pollitt - He was at St Petersburg on business as a representative for the Irwell and Eastern Rubber Company during an outbreak of cholera which rapidly spread through parts of Russia. He travelled on to Warsaw where he became ill and died in hospital on 25th September 1908. He had worked for the company for nearly twenty years and lived at Alder House, Hawthorn Park Wilmslow.

TO THE MEMORY OF
JOHN POLLITT
OF WILMSLOW
WHO DIED AT WARSAW, RUSSIA. SEPT. 25TH 1908
AGED 50 YEARS.
This tablet is erected as a token of affectionate remembrance by his friends.

DEAN ROW CHAPEL GRAVEYARD

Sundial built in memory of the chapel founders in 1871 and restored in 2000. It has bars on the east and west faces to cast a shadow, with the usual sundial on the south side.

Many of the Gregs of Styal are buried here in a large family vault. To avoid flooding there is an underground drain within this and the Worthington grave, which takes the water down to the River Dean.

Hans Renold (1852-1943) was founder of the family engineering firm Renolds Chain. He was Swiss and came to England in 1873 where he was employed as a technical draughtsman and machine inspector. He bought a company in Salford making bicycle chains which he developed into a much larger business with a works in Burnage. By 1930 other firms had merged with his to make it the foremost producer of precision chains in Britain.

His first wife was a descendant of Mrs Gaskell and his second, the daughter of a Unitarian minister. Renolds was a Manchester magistrate and played a leading part in the design of Manchester College of Technology.

Andrew Knox (1814-1886) son of the theologian Alexander Knox. He was an East India Merchant, muslin manufacturer and dyer. In the 1850s he patented improvements in the production of ornamental fabrics.

John Chorlton's grave used to have a large stone over it to prevent grave robbers known as 'resurrectionists' from stealing the body for medical purposes. Following the 1832 Anatomy Act, the medical profession was given legitimate access to cadavers to study.

Chorlton (1813-1880), who lived at Chorlton House, Fulshaw Park had a business at 81 Piccadilly Manchester selling a range of goods which included jewellery, and fishing and archery equipment.

Left: There are also the earlier graves of Rachael Bates of Poynton in 1751 and John Clark 1754.

Left: Thomas Worthington, Manchester architect (1826-1909) designed some of the City's finest buildings including the Crown Court Minshull Street, and the Albert Memorial and Memorial Hall, Albert Square. He was also responsible for Lancaster railway station and Manchester College Oxford.

Worthington was one of the pioneers to design hospitals based on the pavilion system. These were from the ideas he had received in correspondence with his friend Florence Nightingale. He was president of the Royal Manchester Institution and an advisor to the City Art Gallery Committee.

John Williams Morris

minister of the chapel between 1817 and 1843.

In 1827 Morris had a public debate about the merits of Christianity with Richard Carlile, an avowed atheist, reformist and radical campaigner who toured the country expounding his views and challenging the clergy. About 1000 people came to hear the two hour discussion at the chapel. Morris brought along several large books in order to appear learned, but never referred to them. They resumed their debate the following evening at the Unitarian Meeting Room in Stockport.

Dean Row chapel.

Carlisle was nicknamed 'the Devil's Chaplain' for his outspoken condemnation of the church but later converted to Christianity. He was asked to speak at the meeting which later became known as the Peterloo Massacre in 1819. Carlisle managed to escape the yeomanry, and travelled back to London where he published the first eye-witness account of the incident in Sherwin's Weekly Political Register. Morris himself later preached at an open-air service commemorating Peterloo.

Grave stone of the Rev Morris.

Morris was editor of the Macclesfield Courier, Honorary Secretary of the Political Union formed in Macclesfield and a campaigner for the repeal of the Corn Laws. In 1831 he brought Thomas Moore, a surgeon living in Bollin Fee to court at Wilmslow. Moore accused him in a drunken argument of selling him two bodies from the churchyard for dissection. A scuffle ensued and Moore attempted to strike the minister for casting doubt on his professional integrity. The magistrates fined the surgeon two shillings and sixpence and legal expenses.

In 1835, newspapers reported that Morris had invented a new steam engine which would cost much less than comparable engines to operate. Morris caused a stir in the area when it was reported in 1838 that he was urging for a taxation on wives! The women of Dean Row and Stockport gathered in an angry group outside his house to protest. He quickly locked and bolted his doors and spoke to the gathering from an upstairs window, explaining it had been a misunderstanding. It had been due to a printer's error in the North Cheshire Reformer where, as a campaigner for temperance, he had advocated a tax on wine, not wives!

There was an appeal on his behalf in 1838 after he got into financial difficulty following a series of unfortunate circumstances. The trust which had supported him as a minister began to bar Unitarian clergy, then his home and laboratory which had recently been newly furnished for private pupil tuition was burnt down in about 1834. The thatched roof of his house near the King William Inn in Wilmslow had caught fire due to a careless neighbour. Also his wife who taught there became severely ill, and the congregation were too poor to give him anything.

By 1841 Morris seemed to have got back to some financial stability because he was advertising for financial backers for an engine which could be used in mills, factories and mines. He had obtained a patent for an engine which he claimed was cheap to make and would make large revenues. One local said of 'Parson Morris' that many thought kindly of him, and 'whose chief fault was poverty, and no crime is so severely punished'.

A bassoon used in earlier times to accompany the hymn singing.

The River Bollin where it flows through Wilmslow Park.

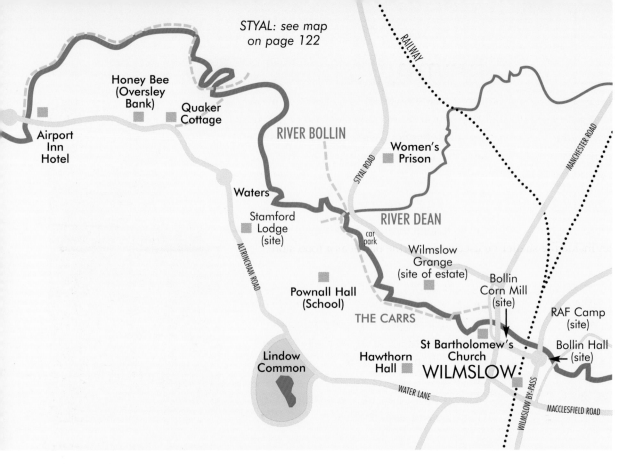

STYAL: see map on page 122

Honey Bee (Oversley Bank)

Quaker Cottage

RIVER BOLLIN

Women's Prison

RAILWAY

MANCHESTER ROAD

Airport Inn Hotel

STYAL ROAD

Waters

Stamford Lodge (site)

car park

RIVER DEAN

Wilmslow Grange (site of estate)

Bollin Corn Mill (site)

RAF Camp (site)

ALTRINCHAM ROAD

Pownall Hall (School)

THE CARRS

Bollin Hall (site)

Lindow Common

Hawthorn Hall

St Bartholomew's Church
WILMSLOW

WILMSLOW BY-PASS

WATER LANE

MACCLESFIELD ROAD

The bridge over the River Bollin in the background leading to the old Bollin Hall, and the mill race to Bollin corn mill in the foreground with the lane also leading to the hall. The site is now covered by the Wilmslow bypass.

'Jarmug'

'Jarmug' was the nickname given to a character, known to many Wilmslow residents, both young and old, who slept rough by the River Bollin. He lived in various temporary shelters in the district including a bacon container with a roof of corrugated iron, and a piano crate, keeping warm by a fire in a battered bucket and wearing several pairs of trousers and coats, although he never wore socks. He transported coal to the sites by means of a two-wheel 'bogey', and got the nickname through drinking out of a jam jar. Inside the shelter he used a margarine barrel as a food store.

Locals ensured he didn't go hungry, and a butcher on Church Street used to give him a parcel of left-over meat each Saturday. He was known by shopkeepers for his requests of a pennyworth of bacon or tea. 'Jarmug' attracted attention in the town as he walked around with a swagger associated with music-hall artists, and always singing to himself. Children found him approachable and some had long conversations with him. But a number of the youngsters took advantage of his innocent nature and played tricks on him.

There are stories of him being persuaded to dress in a bridegroom's suit to get married, and another of him being convinced he was to be the next rector and walking behind the band to church wearing a frock coat and tall hat. Local boys used to push over his bacon-box home, throw stones at his frying pan, and generally harass him until he lost his temper. On another occasion, vandals set fire to his shelter completely destroying it, then others came and made him a new home out of packing cases, covered in oilcloth and sacking.

He spoke in a broad accent which made him difficult to understand, but he told people about the treadmill, presumably at Knutsford prison, on which as he recalled 'you kept going upstairs and never got anywhere'.

'Jarmug,' real name Stephen Beswick, was born in 1848 and lived most of his life with his widowed mother in Wilmslow. At thirteen he was an errand boy living on Old Road, then later worked in the Alderley Edge copper mines. In his thirties he was a labourer at Wilmslow coal wharf, living on Clay Lane. By 1891 he and his mother had moved to Park Road in the Newtown district.

Two years later, probably after his mother's death, he was involved in a disturbing incident at his home. Two teenagers seemed to have befriended him and came to his house where they brutally tortured and killed two of his cats. They were sent to prison by the local magistrate, who described their actions as the most brutal and disgusting he had ever dealt with.

The railway arches over the Bollin where Jarmug spent some of his nights.

Some time after this, Beswick hit hard times and began sleeping rough around the district, initially under the railway arches, perilously close to the River Bollin. Later, some residents allowed him to build shelters on their property, and by 1909 it was reported that he was living in a large back garden at Hill Top. There was concern about him living in such poor conditions but because he was on private land the authorities could not move him without his consent. However, as his health deteriorated, he was persuaded to move to Knutsford workhouse where he died in 1915 aged sixty-seven.

Cheshire Archives & Local Studies

The mill c1949, which used to stand near the corner of Manchester Road and Bollin Walk.

Bollin Corn Mill

William Kitchen (1851-1932) the miller at Wilmslow from 1887, married Emma Bourne in 1877, the daughter of Robert Lindop Bourne a well-known grocer in Wilmslow.

William's father, William, was a corn dealer in Heaton Norris Stockport, before moving to Waterside Marple.

William his grandfather was the inn-keeper of the Orange Tree, Butley, at the junction of London Road and Flash Lane. His ancestors had farmed at Handforth Hall for several generations. After his death at the age of 31 in 1831, his wife Ann continued as licensee for over fifty years until she died in 1883. Her daughter took over the inn for the next eight years before her death in 1891.

Above: Remnant of the Prescot House sign from the house next to the mill where the Kitchens lived
Below Left: William Kitchen
Below right: Robert Kitchen, who ran the mill after his father's death in 1932 until 1949

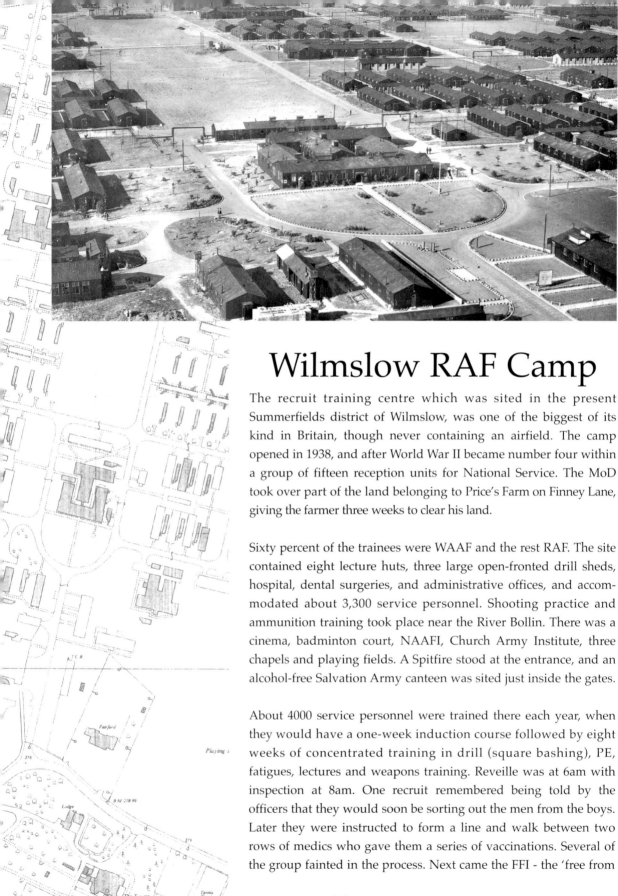

Wilmslow RAF Camp

The recruit training centre which was sited in the present Summerfields district of Wilmslow, was one of the biggest of its kind in Britain, though never containing an airfield. The camp opened in 1938, and after World War II became number four within a group of fifteen reception units for National Service. The MoD took over part of the land belonging to Price's Farm on Finney Lane, giving the farmer three weeks to clear his land.

Sixty percent of the trainees were WAAF and the rest RAF. The site contained eight lecture huts, three large open-fronted drill sheds, hospital, dental surgeries, and administrative offices, and accommodated about 3,300 service personnel. Shooting practice and ammunition training took place near the River Bollin. There was a cinema, badminton court, NAAFI, Church Army Institute, three chapels and playing fields. A Spitfire stood at the entrance, and an alcohol-free Salvation Army canteen was sited just inside the gates.

About 4000 service personnel were trained there each year, when they would have a one-week induction course followed by eight weeks of concentrated training in drill (square bashing), PE, fatigues, lectures and weapons training. Reveille was at 6am with inspection at 8am. One recruit remembered being told by the officers that they would soon be sorting out the men from the boys. Later they were instructed to form a line and walk between two rows of medics who gave them a series of vaccinations. Several of the group fainted in the process. Next came the FFI - the 'free from

94

infection' inspection with all having to lower pants to the knees. Another recruit recalled the first day they were allowed out of camp. First of all he and his friends went to the wrong guard house to show their passes - the WAAFs - which incurred the wrath of the officers, and then spent the next hour and a half doing drill and cleaning uniform before the NCO was satisfied with their smartness and finally allowed them out.

A female recruit remembered the kit they were issued included long dark blue knickers down to the knees nicknamed 'blackouts' which they refused to wear. They were also known as 'harvest festivals'- all is safely gathered in. Kit was given out on the basis of visual assessment with no measuring. Civilian clothes were parcelled up and sent home.

Between 1940 and 1942 the camp was a depot for units and personnel going to Africa, and a base for 75 Maintenance Unit who recovered crashed aircraft in the West Pennines area. One person died of meningitis at the camp and there had also been severe outbreaks of flu and scarlet fever.

A local journalist visited the camp in 1959, following local comments that the recruits did not attend the local youth clubs outside the camp. He reported that the leisure facilities for the recruits was good. Within the three NAAFIs there were jukeboxes, pianos, radios and good food served. The Wilmslow Guild provided lectures and concerts. An 800-yd track at the camp was used by Stockport Motor Club for 'Formula 10' racing-cars that were over ten years old with a capacity up to 1,200cc. This prompted complaints about the noise from locals in 1962.

R.A.F. STATION WILMSLOW.

The final batch of WAAFs trained there in May 1960, and afterwards it was used solely for RAF recruits. The Camp officially closed on 22nd February 1963, but the three longest-serving civilians, who had worked there for twenty years, left a month later and the remaining buildings were put up for auction by the MoD.

Above: Hut no.246, G2 Flight, no.2 Squadron, November 1956. Cpl. Weavers and Cpl. Cadd.

Despite a local petition to keep the old site as a country park it was announced in 1978 that part of the site along with Homestead Farm, had been recommended by the Secretary of State for the building of 700 homes.

Hawthorn Hall

Today the hall is surrounded by housing, but until the 1890s it was situated on open land stretching down to the River Bollin - see the 1875 map on the opposite page.

The earliest reference in around 1200 refers to the place as 'Harethorn', when it was granted by Matthew de Fulscha to the Fitton family of Bolyn, Gawsworth and Pownall. It passed into the ownership of the Pownall family in the 15th century, and they continued to hold it, with references to 'John Pownall of Haythorne' in 1512, and Edmund in 1532. The Hawthorne estates were sold by Henry Pownall to George Latham of Irlam in 1606. His descendant, Captain Thomas Latham, was in Lord Delamere's Volunteer Regiment in 1688 which assisted the Prince of Orange in re-establishing Protestantism. Afterwards the regiment took part in the battle of the Boyne in Ireland, then returned to Wilmslow where they were welcomed back with great rejoicing.

The Hawthorne and Irlam estates were sold about in 1695 to John Leigh, who is thought to have been a London solicitor. The present hall was built by Leigh in 1698, as seen by the date and the initials JL on the lead water spouts, onto an earlier timber structure by John Latham c1610.

After Leigh's death in 1719, his estates were eventually inherited in 1732 by John Page whose grandson, Thomas Leigh Page, sold it at

96

auction in 1799 to Ralph Bower of Wilmslow, a cotton spinner and co-owner with his brother John of 'Handforth' water, corn and cotton spinning mill. It was later known as Carr Mill and created further wealth for the next generation of the Bower family, who owned ninety-six pieces of land around Wilmslow in about 1830.

Hawthorn became a boarding school which had previously been at Green Hall. The school was advertised in 1806 as 'completely detached from any place where the boys might form improper connections...' The classics were taught there, although instruction in French required an additional charge. It cost one guinea to join the school, then 30 guineas board and tuition, and washing 10s 6d per quarter. The headmaster, Mr Fell, advised prospective fee payers that the hall contained many good lodging rooms which meant that the bedrooms were not overcrowded.

By 1819, Mr Nicholson had become the Head and he assured potential school parents that he would give his 'unremitted attention to the health, morals and domestic comfort as well as to their literary instruction' of the 'young gentlemen under his care'. The 'genteel academy' could take twenty-five pupils at the spacious hall and had extensive pleasure grounds.

In 1829 it was the home of Ralph Bower, the son of the mill owner, until he died in 1834. The Bowers were Methodists and attended

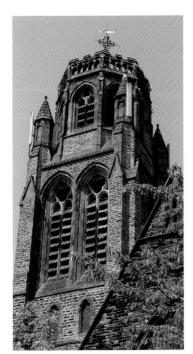

St Paul's Church tower, Heaton Moor, by architect Frank Page Oakley.

the Water Lane chapel. Many visiting preachers from the Stockport circuit were given hospitality at the hall. Bower's family continued to live there for another year, until it became a boarding school for the sons of wealthy Methodists run by former missionary Mr Sutherland.

William Allen lived there until his death in 1840 aged twenty six, then the 1841 census lists Peter Wood, a weaver, and his wife Ann at Hawthorn Hall. Two years later the Hall was advertised to let, including a large walled garden, and seven Cheshire acres of land.

A new classical, commercial and mathematical academy was established at Hawthorn Hall in 1843 by Dr Thomas Somerville for boys between the ages of seven and eighteen. He was previously head of Oakham Academy and held progressive views on education. He did not use corporal punishment and used methods which encouraged pupils to reason out information for themselves rather than just learning 'rules and maxims'. Somerville demanded strict attendance of school hours but with the fundamental principle of kindness as the motivation for learning. Testimonials from parents, teachers and former pupils indicate that he was an effective and amiable teacher. Amongst the wide range of subjects taught were Natural Philosophy and 'Polite Literature'. Fees for pupils under ten were thirty guineas per annum, thirty-five for the over twelves and three guineas for washing.

Thomas Somerville's popularity amongst his pupils is seen by their presentation to him of a writing desk in 1845 with this letter: 'We respectfully beg your acceptance of the accompanying writing desk as a small token of our esteem and gratitude for the unwearied attention you have devoted to our education and for the kindness and consideration which you have exhibited to us. We are, dear sir, Your affectionate pupils.'

There was a tea party at the hall the following year in celebration of the founding of an independent Chapel in Wilmslow on land given by John Jenkins of Plymouth Grove Manchester. The academy had close links with the chapel as it had been established for the sons of Nonconformists (Dissenters) from around the Country. In 1861, there were two pupils from Spain; in 1871 there were scholars from Ireland and the USA. The 1881 Census revealed that there were twenty scholars including one from India, five support staff and four teachers. The notable preacher and theologian Matthew Henry used to stay at the hall while on visits to the area.

The school's success could be seen in 1858 when a third brother in the Cochrane family gained a scholarship to King's College London. Scholars at the school included: (Sir) William Cobbett, the head of a prominent legal practice in Manchester, and instrumental in moving Manchester Infirmary to new premises on Oxford Road; and (Sir) Bosdin Leech, Lord Mayor of Manchester, a key figure in bringing the Ship Canal and water from Thirlmere to the city, and the author of the history of the Manchester Ship Canal.

Dr Somerville died at Hawthorn Hall in 1883 aged 76 and his son-in-law Joseph M'Kim took over the running of the academy. Mr WP Caldwell, who had acted as joint head since 1874, moved to be Principal of Barbourne College, Worcester. The last advertisements for the academy appeared in 1888.

In 1891 the trustees of Ralph Bower sold the hall and grounds for £3500. In 1896 the hall was again up for sale and in danger of being demolished. Wilmslow District Council considered purchasing the building described as 'one of the most ancient buildings of its kind in Cheshire'. The Hawthorn Chapel at Wilmslow Parish church which had also been owned by the Bower family was offered for sale in 1900 and purchased by the church wardens. The four pews brought an annual income of £15. Mr Gladstone, the future Prime Minister, regularly sat in the chapel when a pupil at Wilmslow Rectory.

Frank Page Oakley and family came to the hall in about 1894 and supervised the renovation of the decaying building including the demolition of an old annexe, presumably built to provide extra accommodation during its time as a boarding school. He was an architect in the Arts and Crafts style specialising in churches. Born in 1862 in London the son of Rev John Oakley, Dean of Manchester, his work is to be found both locally and around the world. He became a practising architect in 1886 in Manchester, when his business address was the Deanery. By 1914 he worked at Cross Street, and then at King Street between 1923 and 1926. He contributed two illustrations for JS Crowther's Architectural History of Manchester Cathedral published in 1893, and had worked with Crowther on the restoration and rebuilding of parts of Manchester Cathedral. Oakley lived at Hawthorn Hall until 1904 before moving to Kelsall in Cheshire. He died in Surrey in 1943.

Frank Oakley

1894 Supervised the decoration of St Anne's Church Derby

1895 St Andrew's Church Dearnley

1896 'Uplands' residence Chapel en le Frith

1899 All Souls Church Heywood

1900 Octagonal tower at St Paul's Church, Heaton Moor, thought to be based on St Botolph's Church Lincolnshire, popularly known as the 'Boston Stump'

1901 'Scissor truss' roof at St George-in-the Pines Anglican Church, Banff' Alberta' Canada

1904 St Hilda's Church Old Trafford

1907 Oakley Memorial drill hall at High Wycombe in memory of his brother Rev Roland Oakley, a local curate who died in a motorbike accident.

1908 St Oswald's Church Bollington Cross

1907-8, Eccles Parish Church restoration

1914 St Anne's Brindle Heath, Pendleton

1941 Reredos at St John the Baptist Chester

Katherine Greg and her sister Isabel, daughters of Samuel Greg, who was the son of the founder of Quarry Bank Mill Styal, landowner and magistrate, moved into Hawthorn Hall in 1904. Earlier, Katherine had worked as a district nurse caring for the poor of Liverpool, as well as occasionally working as a support nurse at London Hospital. Katherine and Isabel were animal lovers and involved in the setting up of shelters for lost or starving cats at Cheetham and Hulme in Manchester. She and her sister also provided the money in 1915 for a YMCA recreation room for troops at the Colwyn Bay garrison. Isobel died in 1920, and Katherine in 1934 leaving £1700 to animal charities. She was described as one of a fast disappearing breed of 'Victorian Women' because of her reticence to seek publicity for her good works.

Above: The hall on Hall Road, off Hawthorn Lane, before it was surrounded by high hedges. The gates were probably installed by Frank Oakley in the 1890s during extensive renovations to the building.

Below: Hawthorn Hall , 1970.

In about 1915 an underground passage was discovered by workmen in the grounds of the hall. A large flagstone was lifted to reveal a brick-built room where a felt hat was found lying on the floor. There was speculation this had once led to Pownall Hall. James Muirhead, an engineer involved in waterworks construction, and family came to live at the hall. Next it was the residence of the Simmon family between 1944 and 1959. Hawthorn Hall was converted into offices in 1977. The hall was extensively restored in 2009 and a 1970s extension to the west of the building removed. The manor house is Grade II listed.

Bridle road at the Carrs

The Bollin as it goes under the bridge by the Wilmslow Bypass.

The Wilmslow Grange Estate

The present residential areas of Grange Park Avenue and Bollin Hill stand on the site of the old Wilmslow Grange Estate which was established in the 1850s. Going back over the centuries, Wilmslow or 'Le Bollin' had been under the lordship of the Fitton family but with the death of Hamo Fitton in c1374 it passed through the De Venable family and then divided into Bollin Fee and Pownall Fee in 1421. The Wilmslow lands continued under the ownership of the Booth family and their successors the Greys until parts were sold in the 1850s.

FARM HOUSE

The Tithe map made between 1836 and 1851 shows that most of the future estate area was then co-owned by the Earl of Stamford with two other smaller landowners - Joseph Hulme and Peter Hadshead. The homestead, which would become the site of Wilmslow Grange was occupied by Philip Williams, a farmer, who had use of six fields to the south and west of his home. In 1841, aged fifty, he lived there with his wife Sarah and daughter of the same name.

The farm's co-owner, John Walker Knight, was a farmer near Heald Green who also owned land at Stockport and Northenden, and a one acre close of land at Morley next to the Bollin, known as the Butty Field. Born in Barfield, Essex of Quaker parents, he married Catherine Goodier at the Friends Meeting House, Morley in 1827. The records show that they lived near Heald Green from 1841 until 1851 when he was imprisoned at Chester for non-payment of his tithes - £3 17s 6d. Knight died in 1855 and was buried in the Friends' graveyard in Wilmslow.

THOMAS CHADWICK

In 1853, George Harry Grey, Earl of Stamford, put up his Wilmslow Estate of almost 3000 acres for sale. It was sold off in 141 lots, with Thomas Chadwick, a Manchester estate agent, purchasing eighty two acres which would become known as the Wilmslow Grange estate. 'Grange' sometimes has monastic associations but here it was referring to a gentleman's residence with farm outbuildings. As a surveyor, valuer and arbitrator he was experienced in the business of buying and administrating an estate.

Chadwick was born in Macclesfield in 1818, before the family moved to Salford. His father had been a silk merchant, then later

George Harry Grey
Earl of Stamford.

became an estate agent and accountant in partnership with his son. Thomas married Elizabeth Skelhorn of Salford at St John's Manchester in 1839 and by 1851 he was listed as an estate broker living on Eccles New Road with four children. His brother, David, was also an accountant and MP for Macclesfield for over twenty-five years.

Thomas worked as a partner in his father's company, John Chadwick and Sons, accountants, estate agents and valuers, first at 43 King Street Manchester, and then number 28 from 1842. The partnership was dissolved in 1849 with Thomas taking over the business, and it was then his name which was frequently seen on advertisements for property and land sales. He moved his business to the Clarence Building, on Booth Street close to Albert Square in 1854 and was an agent for the National Mercantile Life Assurance Company.

Chadwick was also chairman of the North Cheshire Water Company, and the Wilmslow and Alderley Edge Gas Company, and director of the Blackpool Tramways Omnibus and Carriage Company. He was secretary of the Albert Benefit Building Society and on the committee of the Ashton-under-Lyne, Stalybridge and North Derbyshire Railway Company. In addition, he owned a mill at Ollerset New Mills, as well as properties in the Adelphi area of Salford. He was a member of both the London and Manchester Estate Exchanges, and in 1869 was appointed by the Board of Trade as an arbitrator in cases involving valuations of land and property. Chadwick was also an accountant and agent of John Clarke Prescott, Manchester merchant and landowner.

Blackfriars Bridge, Manchester.

Thomas was committed to the removal of tolls, and became Secretary of the group which campaigned for the abolition of tolls on Blackfriars Bridge between Manchester and Salford. £8000 was raised by public subscription to buy out the shareholders and the bridge was officially made free to the public in a ceremony on 11th March 1848. Previously, the poor of both cities had been forced to make a diversion across the Victoria Bridge rather than pay the tolls. On the day the tolls were removed someone chalked 'To let' on the toll-keeper's kiosk. There was much rejoicing in the two cities; 1200 loaves were given to the poor in Salford, flags were flown, church bells rang, and the last halfpenny taken as toll was preserved and engraved with the names of the giver and the toll-keeper. In a celebration meeting at Salford Town Hall Chadwick was thanked for his efforts and presented with a silver tea service. In his speech

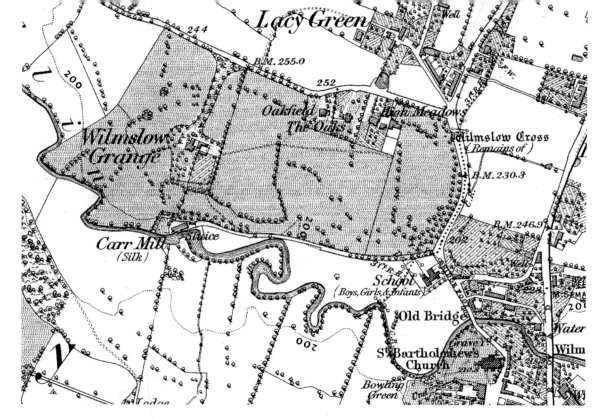

The Grange estate c1875 which included the properties of Oakfield, The Oaks and High Meadows. To the south was Carr silk mill, and the infant school.

of thanks he said that he had always been opposed to toll bridges but wanted them to be removed in a reasonable way which was also fair to the investors.

He was also Secretary of the committee which organised the ending of tolls on Chester Road, Hulme through to the Regent Road Bridge, for foot passengers in 1849 and cattle and traffic in 1855. Chadwick was part of a procession led by a band playing 'See the conquering hero comes'. Afterwards, at the Ellesmere Inn, a crowd of about three hundred gathered to sing 'Rule Britannia' and 'God save the Queen'. The procession then moved on to the Wellington Inn for refreshments and toasts to Chadwick and his committee. Chadwick later presented the last penny taken at the toll to Salford Museum.

By 1858 Chadwick had moved to the newly-built Wilmslow Grange and began using it as an additional business address. The homestead referred to on the Tithe map had been transformed into a substantial house set on an elevated site, with views over the wooded Bollin valley and the hills of Cheshire, Derbyshire and Alderley Edge, and approached by a winding drive from the Styal Road. The house had six bedrooms and was powered by gas throughout.

There were extensive gardens with a fountain, orchard and plantations. Outbuildings included greenhouses, coach house, fowl house, piggeries and granary. There was a spring on the site, and the house was surrounded by trees to ensure privacy from the mill to the south and the Wilmslow to Styal Road to the north. Lacy Green Farm was situated next to the house. The remains of Wilmslow cross stood in a field on the estate near Cliff Road and Styal Road, but today there is no trace of the old monument.

The Grange Estate also received rents from the substantial properties on Styal Road: Oakfield, Oaks and High Meadow, built about 1865 on the site of former cottages, along with the rents from six cottages on the old Manchester to Wilmslow turnpike road, and six cottages on Mill Brow near the Parish Church.

The 1861 Census reveals Thomas and Elizabeth living at Wilmslow Grange with six of their children, Elizabeth's mother, and three servants. Frederick the eldest son, aged fifteen, was a student at Owens College. He married Mary Edith Grundy in 1866 but tragically died in 1871 after contracting rheumatic fever and then a stiff knee which was treated by doses of chloroform. Frederick lost consciousness and died soon afterwards. At the

Changes on the Grange estate between 1875 and 1909 show the new lodge on Styal Road, the extensive glasshouses, a track to the east of the house down to the river, and that the Carr mill had become a laundry in 1903.

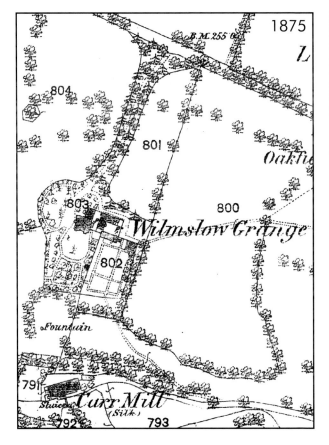

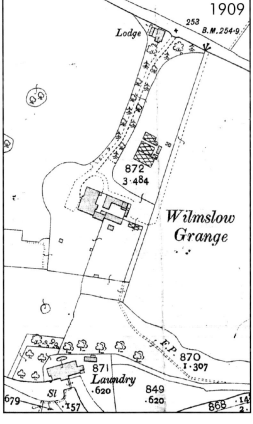

inquest at the George and Dragon Wilmslow, it was found that the doctor had administered what was considered the correct dosage for the condition. Frederick's widow moved back to live with her parents in Whitefield. At the time of his death, Frederick and his brother, Charles, were listed as surveyors and valuers, whilst the next brother, Alfred, was a farmer.

Thomas Chadwick seems to have played an active role in parish affairs, such as the opening of the new school in 1867, and in vestry meetings at the church. By March 1876 he was not in good health. He had made his will, and spent time in the spa town of Harrogate but died on the 27th of December at Wilmslow Grange.

After Thomas's death, the family moved out of Wilmslow Grange and the estate was put up for sale in 1880. Elizabeth, Thomas's widow, went to live with her youngest two children, Rosa and Albert at Rose Cottage, Crofts Bank Road, Dumplington. It was in a rural setting near the River Irwell but the site is now the Trafford Boulevard and near the junction of Old Park Lane, close to the Trafford Centre. Elizabeth and Rosa moved again to Parsonage Road Flixton before Elizabeth's death in 1893 aged seventy-seven.

Within three years of Thomas's death, Charles Henry, his second son, was declared bankrupt. Charles had continued the family business as a land agent and valuer with offices in Manchester and Westminster, but by 1879 he had absconded leaving debts of about £27,000. At a meeting in his absence, the creditors agreed to write off the amount. Charles does not seem to be listed in the 1881 census, but ten years later he had resumed the business as an estate agent in Salford. He died in Ormskirk in 1905. Thomas's other sons Alfred and Albert both worked in insurance.

Wilmslow Grange seems to have remained uninhabited for some years, but the estate and farm were used to sell crops in 1879, heifers in 1883 and horses in 1888. Also in 1881, tenders were requested for a 240-yard long road on the estate.

Dr Alexander Hodgkinson

DR ALEXANDER HODGKINSON

Dr Alexander Hodgkinson became the next resident at the house in 1891. He was co-founder of the Manchester Hospital For Consumption and Diseases in 1875, as well as being its Senior Honorary Physician. He was born in Salford in 1846 and did part of his training at Owens College Manchester and graduated at Edinburgh University. He was a lecturer on diseases of the throat and nose at Owens College, and president of the Laryngological section of the BMA.

Hodgkinson had recently married Eliza Whitnall whose first husband, Arthur Whitnall, had died in 1890. He founded the brewery company Groves and Whitnall at Regent Road, Salford in 1875 along with Eliza's father, William Peer Groves, and her brother, William Grimble Groves. After the death of William Peer, James Groves, brother of William Grimble and Elizabeth joined the board of the company, and they went on to found the Salford Boys' Club in 1903, which provided sports and outdoor pursuits for the youth of the area to help them to become better citizens.

Alexander and Eliza Hodgkinson had four children. Their second son, Alan, was killed during WWl in 1916. Sissie, Eliza's daughter from her previous marriage, died in 1891 just three months after her mother's second marriage. Alexander retired in 1904 and later donated a teaching model of the human head to Manchester University. He had interests in horticulture and had an orchid named after him. Alexander also enjoyed travelling to Australia and North and South America, as well as taking part in many outdoor leisure and sporting pursuits. After his retirement he and Eliza went to live in Farnham in Surrey. Eliza who was born in Melbourne died during a sea voyage in 1926 aged seventy four. They were on the 'Kenilworth Castle' of the Union Castle Line, possibly en route to South Africa. Alexander died two years later, leaving the present-day equivalent of six and a half million pounds in his will.

It was announced in 1922 that a section of the Grange Estate was to be sold off as individual plots in a development known as Bollin Hill. By 1924 some of the houses had been built, and the 1936 OS map shows most plots taken. The Grange itself was occupied by Joseph and Edith Birley between 1918 and 1920. Joseph's great uncle, Hugh Hornby Birley (1778-1845), co-led the Yeomanry who caused the deaths of at least fifteen people and injured at least four hundred at the Peterloo Massacre in 1819. The tragedy gave momentum to the founding of the Chartist movement, the rise of the Trade Unions, and more democratic freedom.

Hugh Birley was also responsible for building one of Manchester's biggest mills. Work began at Cambridge Street in 1814, using cast iron columns and iron framing to construct the six storeys and two basements. 2000 people were employed there spinning and weaving on the 600 looms by the late 1830s. 'Birley's Mill' had been

The Grange c1900

The surving lodge from the Grange estate on the corner of Styal Road and Grange Park Avenue.

mentioned in Engels' 'The Conditions of the Working Class in England'. Birley was also influential in the founding of Owens College and several scientific institutions, as well as being a director of Manchester Gas Works. Charles Mackintosh worked with the Birley family to found his company at the mill in 1824 and bought out the mill in the 1860s to continue producing his famous waterproof goods. The mill was acquired by the Dunlops in 1923.

Joseph's father, Herbert Birley (1821-1890), as well as being a director of an India rubber business in Pendleton, made an outstanding contribution to the development of schools in Manchester and Salford. He gave an estimated £100,000 towards the founding of schools, and was personally involved in the management of up to forty of them. The Birley family were noted for their philanthropy and in 1890 they were described by a local bishop as 'a peculiar people full of good works'. After Herbert's death, medals and prizes were annually awarded in his memory to pupils attending evening schools.

Joseph Herbert Birley

Joseph (1870-1940), who was a Special Constable during WW1, worked at the mill as a departmental manager, and was a councillor in the city where he chaired the Finance and Education committees. He held roles with the Manchester and Salford Savings Bank and the Manchester branch of the Diocesan Association of Church Schools, and was a trustee of St Philip's Church Salford.

His wife Edith (1880-1976) became a JP in about 1950, served on the Manchester Education Committee and was chair of the Probation Committee and Juvenile Court Panel. In 1950 she received an honorary MA from Manchester University for her service to the community. She remained active in public life into her nineties, and was known within the family for her love of knitting, and the inevitable present of woollen socks at Christmas.

Edith Birley

The Grange was occupied by William and Emily Renshaw from 1921 to 1931. William's father owned a flax-spinning works in Broughton which went into voluntary liquidation in 1914. William listed himself as a cotton merchant in 1911. Emily's father, Harvey Heywood, a JP with a dyeing and bleaching business in Middleton, was the town's first Mayor in 1886. In 1933, the house and the remaining 27 acres were put on sale and were still unsold four years later. The Grange could be seen on the 1954 Ordnance Survey map but by 1960 the house had been demolished and the site had become the Grange Park Avenue residential area.

St Bartholomew's Church, Wilmslow.

Cliff Road, on the eastern boundary of the Grange Park estate.

109

Lindow Common

It was the scene of a prize-fight or pugilist encounter between Charley Jones and Gilbert Freeland from Manchester for a prize of £50 in 1836. A big crowd gathered on Easter Monday to watch the fight which lasted over ninety minutes and sixty rounds. Jones did enormous damage to his opponent, whose main tactic was to tumble over to avoid further punishment. Such fights were illegal but the county police could not muster enough numbers to prevent them taking place. In 1840 there was a fight here to settle a quarrel between the son of the owner of the Swan Inn and a local farmer's son. After the contest of over sixty rounds the publican's son was brought home unconscious and died a few hours later. The victor was taken into custody and a verdict of manslaughter was returned at the inquest.

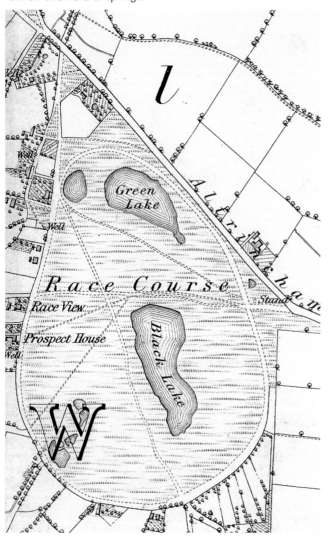

Lindow Common c1875. Black Lake's name is derived from its dark coloured peat stained water. The water came from both rainfall and natural springs.

Racecourse Road which surrounds the common was created by gypsies as a race track to show off their horses in a horse trading event similar to Appleby Fair. It took place during the Wakes which was the last week of August, and was considered by some to bring undesirable elements to the neighbourhood. Gypsies had been coming to Lindow since the Middle Ages and many had settled in the district. An 1806 handbill announced that the annual three cattle markets would take place that year in March, May and November.

By 1810 the Wilmslow Meeting was well established over three days in the September with the races starting each day at 4pm for a £50 purse. The races were mostly three times round the one-mile course. At the bottom of the handbill for that year there were many competitions for the spectators to enjoy including pig races, snuff-taking, whistling, 'smoaking', pudding eating and knitting. The handbill also stated there would be the usual 'Cockings' and 'Ordinaries' at the meeting which referred to draught beer, and meals at fixed prices, being served.

COUNTY OF CHESTER.

WILMSLOW Meetings.

NOTICE TO THE PUBLIC.

THE MEETINGS at the above Place will be held on the following Days in each Year, (unless they happen to fall on a *Sunday*, then to be held on the Day following), viz.

On the 23rd day of March,
The 7th day of May, and } ANNUALLY.
The 15th day of November,

The PREMIUMS to be given to Persons bringing Cattle, &c at the first Meeting, are as follow :

	£	S.	D.
For the best Stallion, of the Draught kind -	2	2	0
---- the best Mare or Gelding, Draught kind -	1	1	0
---- best Colt, rising 3 years old -	1	1	0
---- best Colt, rising 2 years old -	1	1	.0
---- the greatest Quantity of Horned Cattle (one Concern) produced, on Sale -	3	3	0
---- best in-calf Cow exposed to Sale, and sold at a fair price -	1	1	0
---- best Bull produced the first Meeting -	1	1	0
---- best Barren Cow exposed to Sale, and sold at a fair price -	1	1	0
---- best in-calf Heifer, ditto ditto -	0	10	6
---- best one year old Calf, ditto ditto -	0	10	6
---- best Herd of Swine -	1	1	0

N.B. All DISPUTES that may arise respecting any of the PREMIUMS, to be determined by a proper Person, appointed by the Committee for that purpose ; which Determination shall be final.
Dated MARCH 14th, 1806.

Northall and Dawson, Printers, Stockport.

WILMSLOW Meeting.

On Tuesday, September 4th, 1810,
Will be run for, on

Lindow Common,

The *LADIES' PURSE*, not exceeding Fifty Pounds, by Galloways not more than 14 hands high, the best of three two-mile Heats, to carry a Feather.

On Wednesday, Sept. 5, 1810,

The *GENTLEMAN's SUBSCRIPTION PURSE*, value not exceeding Fifty Pounds, by any Horse, Mare, or Gelding, that never won a Fifty Pound Plate, the best of three 3-mile Heats, to carry not less than Eight Stone, unless agreeable to the Stewards, or such Persons as they shall appoint.
On the same Day will be a *MATCH RACE*, by Mr. Turner's b. c. by Sir Oliver, and Mr. Hobson's c. h. Choice.

On Thursday, THE TOWN PURSE,

Value not exceeding Fifty Pounds, by any Horse, Mare, or Gelding, that never won a Fifty Pound Plate, the best of three 3-mile Heats, three times round the Course to a heat, to carry not less than Eight Stone and a half, unless agreeable to the Stewards.
On the same Day, the Gentleman's Sweepstakes of Ten Guineas each will be run for, each Gentleman to ride his own horse.

N.B. No less than three Horses to start for any of the above Plates, unless agreeable to the Stewards. Disputes (if any arise) to be determined by the Stewards.

The Horses will start each Day precisely at 4 o'clock.

There will be ASSEMBLIES, Cockings & Ordinaries
AS USUAL.

Also on each Day, in addition to the above, there will be Wheelbarrow and Pig Races, Quoiting, Cricket, Wrestling and Sparring, Dipping, Whistling, Jumping, Smoaking, Knitting, Bobbing, Bowling, Dancing, Singing, Snuff-taking and Pudding-eating.

J. Dawson, printer, Bridge-street, Stockport.

By 1838 all the races were twice round the course and generally for a prize of fifty sovereigns. There was a fatal accident in 1842 when a rider fell from his horse and was trampled as he was dragged for fifty yards. The mill owner, Mr Greg, had requested soldiers to attend one of the meetings to prevent rioting.

The Wilmslow meeting drew spectators by train from Manchester who paid 3s. first class and 2s. second to attend the two-day event in 1845. The lessee of the Bull's Head advertised for customers describing the town as 'Built in a vale, Sweet Wilmslow greets the eye...eleven arches cross the Bollin stream, And Trafford's Lord gave the town a name'. Another attraction that year for the betting public was a foot race between two local lads over Lindow Common.

There was disapproval from parts of the press in 1856 when there were two 'performances' at the race meeting of the execution of William Palmer who had been hanged at Stafford in the June of that year. The re-enactment had been organised by the landlord of the King's Head Inn. A death mask of the prisoner was attached to a model of the body with the original executioner and other officials re-enacting the hanging.

Above: 1810 handbills
Below: One of the many paths across the Common.

The Common has been designated a nature reserve and Site of Special Scientific Interest where wildlife is supported and protected.

John Royle JP

Memorial plaque which states that Alderman John Royle purchased the Common from the Countess of Stamford and Sir Humphrey De Trafford in 1897 for the residents of Wilmslow. The plaque below commemorates the restoration of the Common as a nature reserve in 1988.

In 1868 a good crowd watched the three races on the first day - the Tradesmen's Plate, the Wilmslow Park Handicap and the Manchester Cup. The next day there were races for the Stewards' Cup, Trafford Park Handicap and the Stockport Stakes. The final meeting on the Common was held in 1872. Lindow Common was also used for rifle shooting competitions between army teams. In 1869 the 27th Cheshire CRN narrowly beat the 1st Company MRV as they shot at targets at distances of 200 and 500 yards. Further contests were reported between 1871 and 1874.

By 1858 the owners of the Common, the Earl of Stamford and Sir Humphrey de Trafford, were agreeable to it being purchased to become a park for Wilmslow. Part of the 48 acres was to be used as a cemetery, with the rest to include gardens, cricket ground, museum, lecture room, gallery and lettable pasture land. The park would be administered by a committee comprised of the two lords of the manor, the rector of Wilmslow, and eighteen trustees. The £1000 required for fencing, drainage and preparing the land for farming was to be raised through a complicated system of shares.

In 1896 there were still concerns that the land owners might enclose the Common and a Council committee was delegated to meet representatives of the lords of the manor to suggest that up to 20 acres of the Common should be given to Wilmslow. The Council sought to re-assert their claim on the common by placing seating at various points, but these were removed by the owners. The following year after a petition was sent from the local ratepayers' association, Wilmslow District Council made an offer of £500 for 50 acres of land which was accepted by the owners. The acquisition of Lindow Common would celebrate Queen Victoria's Diamond Jubilee.

Then in a special meeting, the Chairman of the Committee announced that John Royle (1836-1915), a Wilmslow resident, had offered to buy the Common and donate it to Wilmslow. This generous gesture was received with great applause and hearty thanks by the meeting. It meant that the Common would be protected from all 'encroachments' of the caravan dwellers; although in 1907 the District Council were forced to further enclose the two-acre Fulshaw Recreation Ground to prevent travellers camping there and cattle straying onto the land. This arrangement did not seem to stop public gatherings on the Common, because a public auction of household goods was held there in 1918. Royle was Lord Mayor of Manchester, and involved with many charities and institutions including the Lewis Epileptic Colony, Henshaw's

Blind Asylum, and the Royal Infirmary and Ancoats Hospitals. He founded a successful wholesale boot business in Manchester and also served on the Local Boards of Knutsford and Wilmslow. In addition he helped to found the Anti-Gambling League and served on the Council of Manchester University, as well as being a prominent Liberal politician in Manchester and Knutsford. He was a staunch Wesleyan and in a long and active public life he was highly regarded by everyone who knew or worked with him. After his death, Wilmslow Council decided to erect a memorial to him at Lindow Common in 1921.

Since it had been opened to the public, the lakes became popular with ice skaters. The waters were shallow which meant a minimum of danger if the ice cracked, and skating often continued into the evening by moonlight. The lakes were also a draw for model boat enthusiasts with crowds coming to watch the competitions between model yacht clubs. The lakes, however, gradually became tipping grounds and in 1924 Wilmslow residents drew up a petition to demand the end of tipping by the Council. But nearly ten years later, tipping continued on the Common, and a petition was sent to the Minister of Health urging the local council to change their methods.

By 1932, the Green lake and a smaller lake to the east had received so much refuse that the water had receded and they had been filled in. A set of smaller ponds in the southwest corner of the common had gone by 1965. In May 1958 water from the River Bollin had to be pumped into Black Lake to raise its levels. The following year the waters receded again and 100 fish including five pike were rescued from the lake by the local angling society. In about 1985 the lake was in danger of silting up again with rubbish and weeds before the authorities organised a clean-up and the lake bed was lined with water-tight benonite clay.

The Lake was once a popular place for skating, model boats and fishing.

Parts of the Common were deliberately set on fire in May 1915, and in August 1924 the local council announced it would prosecute anyone found destroying or stealing heather, following years of large quantities being removed.

The Lake has become the habitat of rarely-seen water voles, and where vast numbers of toads spawn.

Stamford Lodge

Now the Waters Corporation offices but previously the site of the Stamford Lodge estate which extended to the banks of the Bollin. An estate map of 1781 shows a building here but it is not clear whether this is Stamford Lodge. However, the Lodge is clearly indicated on the Tithe map of around 1840 when it was owned by the Earl of Stamford and occupied by John Goodier, who had several farms and many properties in the area. He was a Guardian of the Poor and a Liberal in politics. By 1855 he was in financial difficulty and the farm stock and house contents were auctioned.

In 1851, Jonathan Bailey an assistant overseer lived there, followed by Fenton Atkinson, a Manchester attorney who had defended Luddites in 1812 and 1817. He was described at the time as 'an able lawyer and a thorough hater of oppression, whose legal knowledge and earnest love of liberty were used on behalf of the illegally oppressed.' He was one of the founders of Manchester Law Library which opened at Marsden Street in 1820. Atkinson moved to Didsbury in about 1858.

John Hyde, gentleman, resided at the Lodge in 1861, then John Port by 1874. Port owned an iron bedstead and safe works in Ancoats, Manchester as well as farming the 30-acre Stamford Lodge estate. By 1891 he was in Didsbury until his death in 1903, when he left the equivalent of about £50 million in his will, including the former Fulshaw Hall estate, and buildings and land in Manchester.

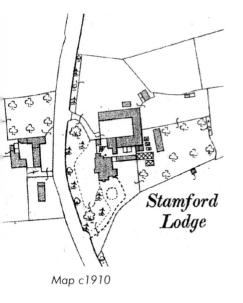

Stamford Lodge

Map c1910

Stamford Lodge was advertised for sale by John Port in 1883, described as a good house with four entertaining rooms, seven bed-rooms, good farm buildings, and with no restrictions for further building on the 44-acre site without affecting the privacy of the Lodge. It was possibly Port who had extended the Lodge during his time of ownership, as the 1874 OS map indicates there had been extensions to the north-east of the building shown on the Tithe map.

Francis Godlee, a cotton cloth manufacturer and calico printer with the firm Simpson and Godlee, moved to Stamford Lodge in 1892 and lived there for nearly thirty years. He used to drive to work in a dog-cart to catch the early train at Wilmslow station with such regularity that people could set their clocks as he passed by. He was keen on punctuality and Stamford Lodge contained many clocks, including one which kept perfect 'astronomical' time.

114

Godlee was the son of a Quaker barrister in London and spent most of his life helping others. He and friends founded the Hugh Oldham Lads' Club, one the earliest of its kind, in Manchester, and regularly attended its gatherings and meetings, as well as supporting a Quaker school in Yorkshire where he donated the money for a swimming pool. In Manchester, he was involved with the University, the College of Technology, later UMIST, Ancoats Hospital and the Manchester and Salford Trustee Savings Bank.

He liked to have the latest technology, with the first electric lighting in the district, the fourth telephone in Wilmslow, and X-ray equipment which he used to photograph his friends' hands. Godlee presented an observatory and telescopes to the City at a cost of £10,000. His other interests included cycling, breeding horses and boating in Scotland.

In business, he was known as a sympathetic employer yet with good business acumen and became chairman of the successful firm in 1914. By 1918 he had moved to 'Harefield' which later became the northern headquarters of ICI, possibly because he needed more space for all his equipment and increasing possessions. He was not in good health by then and retired from business in 1924 with his nephew taking over. He was known as a courteous person if rather shy, with a dislike for music and all forms of hypocrisy. He remained a committed Quaker all his life and when he died in 1928 in his 74th year, the funeral was at the Friends' Meeting House, Wilmslow.

The observatory presented by Francis Godlee in 1903 is situated at the University of Manchester's Sackville Street building. It is open to the public with guided tours, workshops and talks. The website of the Manchester Astronomical Society gives access arrangements and details of forthcoming events.

Below: The observatory can be seen on top of the roof on the left hand side. The building at the time of its official opening in 1902 was the Manchester Municipal Technical School.

Walter Lee Cooper, co-owner with his brother of a bus fleet, came to live at Stamford Lodge. By 1928, it was the home of Sir Norris Agnew, a solicitor born in Pendleton who had previously lived at Warford Hall, and was still listed at the Lodge in 1939. He was knighted for his services to St Mary's and the other Manchester hospitals. He practised as a solicitor until 1952 when he devoted himself to public works up to his death in 1977.

By 1978, Ciba-Geigy and Huntingdon Life Sciences who had taken over the site announced plans to extend the labs. They were involved in pharmaceutical testing on animals, and were moving staff from Horsham HQ to work here. In 1983 animal rights protesters tried to break into the site following rumours that rodents and dogs were being tested to establish the toxicity of fly sprays. Officials at the company declined to reveal which tests were taking place but stated they operated under a Government licence and that the testing was decreasing. There was an explosion and fire at the site in 1983 causing £10,000 damage but no serious injuries. Campaigners continued to target the company and in 1998 the site with its forbidding high fence was closed.

An American company, Waters Corporation based in Massachusetts acquired it in 2011 to build a new £60 million 'dream office park' HQ within the 34-acre site set in Green Belt land. The historic Stamford Lodge and gardens, the home of philanthropists and reformers, which had been originally planned to be refurbished within any developments, was demolished to make way for the mass spectrometry research centre.

Quaker cottage

This was the old Friends' Meeting House built in 1693 when the first monthly meeting was held there. Before then, local Quakers had met in each other's homes around Mobberley including Yarwood House farm. The Friends' records in the area date from 1654 to 1831, and there is a burial ground at Graveyard Farm Mobberley. The Quakers were persecuted by the authorities, and in 1665, troopers broke into a house meeting in Mobberley to arrest eighteen worshippers. They and their friends suffered imprisonment and harassment over the following months. Food had to be passed to them through the prison windows. A new Friends' Meeting House on Altrincham Road Wilmslow was opened on 4th June 1831 on land sold for £1 by the Earl of Stamford. The original Meeting House became cottages, later converted into one dwelling, but in 1962 the cottages were under threat of demolition.

The Chapel House

Oversley Bank

Richard Cobbett Jr

This was the home of Richard Cobbett, solicitor and farmer, for about fifteen years. He was the son of William Cobbett, political reformer, journalist and agriculturalist, and perhaps best known for his book 'Rural Rides' which examined poverty in the countryside in the 1820s. Richard was a practising solicitor at Cobbett, Wheeler and Cobbett in Manchester for thirty-five years, and President of Manchester Law Society. He shared many of his father's views and represented Chartists and other radicals. His father wrote a book on French grammar which was presented in the form of letters addressed to 'My Dear Richard', reflecting the warm friendship he enjoyed with his sons. Richard died at Oversley in 1875.

The Honey Bee restaurant

It was briefly the home of Philip Berry, who owned the King's Arms in Spring Gardens Manchester, until his death in 1877. He and his family had lived in Cheadle, and by 1881 his wife Lavinia was the owner of the Midland Hotel, Buxton. Susanna Watson and family had moved to Oversley Bank about 1881. Her husband, Charles, was a cotton merchant born in Charleston USA. By 1901 they had moved to Birkenhead.

Richard Cobbett Jr was living at Oversley Bank in 1906. Like his father, he was a partner in the firm of solicitors Cobbett Wheeler and Cobbett of Manchester and Wilmslow. He was a major in the 5th Battalion Cheshire Regiment, and commanding officer for the Territorial forces of the Wilmslow district, and a local councillor. He died aged 59 in 1913 in a Manchester nursing home. Henry Philips Greg resided at Oversley Bank from 1913 before moving to Lode Hill, Styal by 1919.

Charles Boddington, chairman of the family brewery at Strangeways, Manchester moved to Oversley Bank in 1924 following his marriage to Edith Agnew, whose family had lived there from about 1921. Charles listed himself in 1939 as head brewer and farmer. He died in 1982 and Edith was there until her death in 1990. The property's frontage had been extended to the west in the 1930s, possibly during the ownership of the Boddingtons. Since then it has been a home for the elderly, a hotel, and pub before becoming the Honey Bee pub restaurant.

The Airport Inn

The hotel, previously known as the Valley Lodge, Wilmslow Moat House and Holiday Inn Airport Hotel, stands on the site of Valley House, an old property on the banks of the River Bollin at Oversley, next to the Oversleyford bridge. The bridge had been rebuilt in around 1802 and again in 1872, at a cost of over £1000 following flooding in the valley after the Macclesfield canal burst its banks. Further repairs were carried out in 1879.

In the 1830s Valley House was occupied by William Frankland a farmer and shop-keeper. After his death in 1878 he was buried in the Quaker graveyard in Wilmslow. By 1851 it was the home of Mary Ann Barker, the wife of a shipping merchant, then in 1871 Mark Carter , a tin plate maker at Red Bank, Manchester lived there. with his family. After his death in 1876, the house went up for sale and was advertised as having over four acres of grounds, well-stocked fruit gardens, three bedrooms, stabling for two horses, piggery, fields and pasture land.

Humphrey Dyson

Frank Edmondson, an engraver, lived at Valley House until 1884, then it came into the ownership of Samuel Dyson of Old Trafford. He was followed by his son Humphrey, a grocer at Rochdale Road Manchester, a Wilmslow councillor and involved in promoting the Manchester Ship Canal Bill through Parliament. Humphrey died on Christmas Day 1904.

John Tweedale, a hydraulic packer and cotton merchant at Chorlton Mills, Hulme resided there by 1909. He was also secretary of the North of England Pomeranian Club. In June 1931, the area was hit by a whirlwind which caused trees in the valley to bend and Valley House to shake for ten minutes. The following year the family were rocked by financial difficulties when Tweedale was declared bankrupt, after the failure of his investment of £5000 in the 1930 British 'talkie' 'Piccadilly Nights'- a film set in the world of music hall. The house had to be sold and the contents auctioned.

Between 1936 and 1951, Valley House was owned by the Manchester Clarion Cycling Club who moved from Handforth to hold their meetings and events there. Hubert Humphreys, later the Mayor of Birmingham, officially opened the new premises, and a crowd of six hundred sang 'The Red Flag'. The site was described as quiet and secluded and surrounded by tall trees. There were extensive gardens with large open spaces for football and cricket as well as tennis courts and a putting green.

Above: Valley House c1900
Below: The Bollin at Oversley

In 1938 the house was used for a rally by the Left Bank Club to stage Clifford Odet's play 'Waiting For Lefty' by the Left Theatre Guild, which was about American cab drivers preparing to go on strike. The following year, the National Cyclists' Union held a rally at Valley House with nationally-known cyclists addressing the mass meeting. The Clarion Club eventually sold the property because they could not afford its maintenance, and it became the home of Jack Fletcher, a motorcycle and bicycle dealer in Ashton under Lyne.

In 1952 the grounds had been used by the Central Council of Physical Recreation for two weekend courses in canoeing on the River Bollin, with the British Women's slalom champion amongst the instructors. That same year, land to the north of Valley House was allowed to be used as a caravan site, providing they were used for leisure purposes, unless approved by the Council. The licences had to be renewed after three years. This was one of two licensed sites in Wilmslow, (the other was at Moss Lane Styal) and by 1963 sixty people lived on the site.

Valley House underwent a change of use by 1957 becoming a club, but had been unsuccessful in obtaining an extended licence to sell drinks to airport and airline staff working late hours. Three years later it had been converted into a hotel offering 'soft lights and sweet music' at Saturday evening dances at 5s per person. In a 1962 advertisement the management, Sydney and Tutzy Stone, invited

guests to a Saturday dinner dance where they could 'relax in the atmosphere of charm that pervades the beautiful seventeenth-century house'. When it was put up for sale in 1969, it had a cocktail bar, pickled haggis bar, a restaurant for sixty, and fifteen bedrooms.

The hotel was demolished in 1971 to make way for the Valley Lodge Hotel which had opened by August 1973. Advertisements depicted the new hotel being close to the airport and Tyrolean in style with sixty eight bedrooms. It was further extended in 1983. In 1978, the hotel was promoting the Valley Lodge Singles Club where 'you could meet old and new friends in the finest facilities in Cheshire'. The target market was 'mature and sophisticated' over-25s.

Later the basement club was refurbished and opened as the Equivino nightclub but this was not a success. It was replaced by 'Peruvia', a more glamorous venue which attracted not only people from the surrounding area but also from all over the UK. The exotic dancers, erotic images projected onto the walls and fur-lined toilets helped to attract hundreds of clubbers including tv soap actors, pop stars and Manchester footballers. The car park used to be full of expensive vehicles on club nights. However the Moat House group, owners of the hotel, were concerned that the club had also become a popular venue for Manchester's criminal fraternity and, after trying to solve the problems caused by the gangs, they closed 'Peruvia' in about 1998.

There's a piece of the Austrian Tyrol nestling in a Cheshire Valley, just minutes from Manchester Airport.

It's the NEW Tyrolean-styled

Valley Lodge HOTEL

+ 68 Bedrooms with every modern amenity.
+ Only a few minutes from Manchester Airport and Motorway link.
+ Superb Cuisine in our International Restaurant.
+ Four Bars of highly original, unusual decor.
+ Modern luxury in a traditional hunting lodge atmosphere.
+ Facilities for Conferences and Seminars.

Top: Footpath to Styal along the Bollin next to the Airport Hotel. Above: 1973 Valley Lodge advertisement.

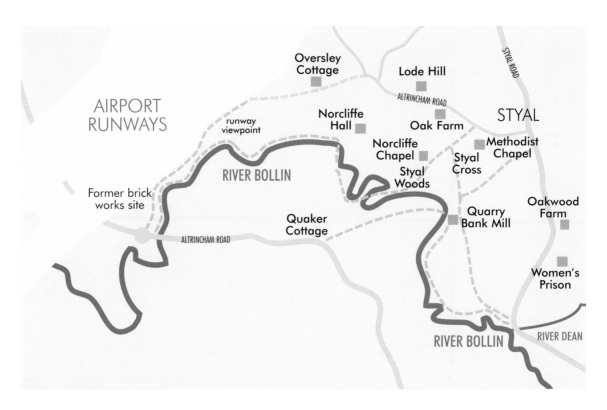

The Bollin near the Carrs, Wilmslow.

STYAL

Above: Styal Road, when it was safe to walk in the middle of the highway.

Right: The River Dean where it joins the Bollin at Wilmslow. In the 1800s the River Dean was referred to as a branch of the Bollin. In 1829 it was reported that the River Bollin had flooded in Bollington destroying eight bridges, and causing damage to cotton factories and homes. In the storms of winter 1877 the yard of the Queen's Inn Bollington collapsed into the river named as the Bollin. A servant girl was flung into the waters but was happily rescued unhurt.

Styal Cottage Homes.

Styal Women's Prison

It was officially opened by the Home Secretary Henry Brooke MP in October 1962 as a semi-secure prison for 247 women at a cost of £260,000. This was to release extra prison accommodation at Strangeways Manchester for men and provide more appropriate accommodation for women at Styal. The prisoners were housed in groups of twenty within thirteen houses, each having a dining room and common room. They learned domestic skills, including the use of sewing machines, laundry work, gardening, decorating and could attend evening classes.

Since its opening, the prison now holds young offenders and has a wing for unsentenced female prisoners. A recent development has been the opening of The Clink Restaurant in 2015 where the food is prepared and served by women prisoners in the former chapel.

For nearly sixty years, the prison site was previously the Cottage Homes for destitute children. It was owned by Chorlton Poor Law Union Board Manchester, and opened in 1898. At the time it was regarded as innovatory with the children housed in detached villas with a 'home mother' in a rural situation, rather than being placed in huge overcrowded barrack-like workhouses. Mary Sale who was closely involved in the women's suffrage movement, was chair

124

of the committee which looked after the welfare of the children until her death in 1929. Emmeline Pankhurst was amongst those involved in the formation of the colony. Styal Homes was only for Protestant children. Catholic boys went to Buckley Hall near Rochdale and the girls to Holly Mount, Tottington.

Initially there were twelve houses for 'Pankhurst's sunshine children' on the 300-acre site but more were added in 1903 and 1927. Edward Hyde Greg at Quarry Bank Mill was against the Cottage Homes and complained Styal would be 'contaminated' by the presence of the workhouse paupers. He planted poplar trees on the boundary of his estate to block out the view of the homes.

Edward Hyde Greg

Quarry Bank Mill Archive, National Trust

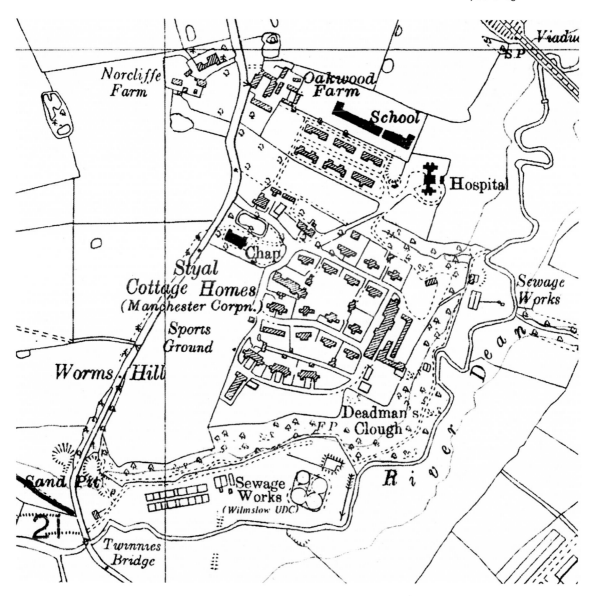

The community was self-contained with a school farm and a system of bulk buying for clothing and other items. They had their own swimming pool, hospital, church, bakery, laundry, recreation hall and workshops. Newcomers were quarantined in the Probationer's Lodge for two weeks before they were admitted into the homes. It was originally planned that the children would attend local schools but the local council refused to admit them due to the influence of Edward Hyde Greg, and so a school was built on the site.

The model village was designed by Manchester architect James Broadbent (1864-1917) who was also responsible for the extension to the Imperial Hotel Blackpool, the Salford Town Hall annexe and a pavilion at Withington Hospital. Broadbent's design for the new Manchester Masonic Hall, Bridge Street was approved in 1915. Building was delayed because of the First World War, and in 1929 his design was replaced by Percy Scott Worthington's more contemporary version.

Original design for the Manchester Masonic Hall by James Broadbent.

At its peak, there were 629 children in 36 cottages, which was more than the population of Styal village. The cost of £50,000 was met with a loan from Liverpool Corporation. The sexes were originally segregated but were later mixed in 1951 to be more like ordinary families. Many of the teenage boys were recruited into the armed services and there is a memorial at Styal Methodist chapel to those who died in the two world wars. Some of the children were sent off to live in Canada to ease the financial burden on Manchester. Before they left, they were each presented with a new shilling. Former pupils recall the harsh methods of the head who was nicknamed 'Smiggy', and others remembered how punishments were given for

Cottage Homes c1914

Wish you were here? 1947 postcard.

the slightest things. This rhyme of the period reflected what some
children thought about the school:

'This time tomorrow we shall be

Out of the gates of misery

No more sorrow, no more pain

No more taste of Smiggy's cane'

However others enjoyed living in the countryside setting and being
able to see fields and cottages from the classroom. The countryside
air also helped to improve the health of some of the children. One
of those who came to the Homes as a 'delicate' child later had
a career in outdoor pursuits.

Olga Hertz (1851-1946) was chairman of the Cottage Homes for five
years. She had devoted her life to serving the poor and needy
in Manchester. She corresponded for over fifty years with many
of the girls who had been brought up at Styal. This included some
who settled and married in Canada. She founded a branch of the
Girls' Friendly Society, and colleagues continued to keep in contact
with the children of the Styal girls who were known as 'Miss Hertz's
Grandchildren'.

The facilities at Styal were likened to those at a public school but
there was little privacy, and some pupils hid possessions in
the walls of the homes. There were many instances of children
absconding from Styal. Outside school activities included a Church
Lads' Brigade band which later became part of the King's Cadet
Corps of the Royal Rifle Regiment. Others joined the Styal Homes
Band which played at many charitable events.

In 1930 responsibility for the children passed to Manchester Education Committee. During the war period the children did not go away on holiday and a new committee took over in 1948 which aimed to improve conditions. In 1949, children up to five years old received 3d spends and 4oz of sweets a week, and fifteen-year olds were given 3s. That same year, the 'Last Post', signifying bedtime and lights out was sounded by a bugler for the last time, because all the school's brass instruments were sold to another school.

From 1951 the City Council began to gradually close down the outdated institution and by July 1956 the children had been dispersed in groups of up to eight in purpose-built 'family' homes around Manchester. It was calculated that about 25,000 children had been at the Cottage Homes during its existence.

The prison chapel, now the venue for The Clink restaurant.

In December the cottage homes were occupied by about fifty families of Hungarian refugees who had fled the revolution. Although great attempts were made to help them settle, the 380 refugees were not happy about the running of the camp. Following a meeting between themselves and Manchester Corporation in 1957 the commandant resigned. Their stay was temporary because many wanted to emigrate to Canada or USA, and all of the refugees had left by 1959.

On the north of the site there was an open-air residential special school for 'delicate' children in poor health. Across the country before the Second World War, the authorities were concerned about the spread of tuberculosis, so many schools were built with an emphasis on good ventilation and more activities taking place outdoors. This was run by Manchester Education Committee from 1936 until its closure in 1995 when it was known as Bollin Cross School. The hospital and the houses nearby have been demolished and the Cottage Homes site was sold for £70,000 to the Home Office prison authority.

128

The Longhorns 'Mars' and "Major" were trained as working animals by the Bollin Valley Partnership to pull a cart. They were often seen on training outings around Styal and at events such as ploughing matches and school fetes. The cart had been purchased from a milkman in Dukinfield. The photograph from the 1990s at the Bollin Valley Partnership's Oakwood Farm shows them being led by Tim Harding, the present head of the Partnership. The cattle have since been sold to the Shakespeare Birthplace Trust.

Hollin Lane, Styal.

129

Quarry Bank Mill

Isaac Hewitt, estate worker

Joseph Acton was the caretaker of the mill from the early 1900s. He lived at the caretaker's lodge and was also the unofficial head gardener. He brought food to prisoners of war who were working at the mill and clearing mud from the mill channels. He remembered the General Strike of 1926, when there was a coal shortage at the mill and a complete floor was cut up to provide fuel. He also recalled the near tragedy when a man fell into the River Bollin and was dragged by the force of the water through the mill's sluice gate. Fortunately he escaped unharmed but worried what his wife would say after losing his hat which was a present from her.

It was announced in October 1959 that the National Trust would take over the mill. Production would stop with the loss of three weavers' jobs. The manager, Samuel Henshaw, who lived at the Apprentice House, stayed on as custodian assisted by his secretary Mrs B Slater. Work had declined in recent years and the remaining workers were producing dish cloths.

Estate workers - photograph of lady by Robert Greg.

Work on the sluice gates after the flood in 1872.

Watercolour by Caroline Greg of a rope bridge by Folly Bridge in Styal Woods. She was the daughter of Robert Hyde Greg of Norcliffe Hall and made many drawings and paintings of Styal. She travelled widely and expressed disappointment in her diaries that she had not married. She died in 1865 aged 37.

Styal Woods

The woods today are a beautiful, peaceful place to enjoy, but in the 1790s they became a place of danger. Some of Samuel Greg's workers had been assaulted in the woods and reward posters were put up in the district. But there was another threat from dangerous armed characters roaming the woods. They were soldiers returning from the Napoleonic wars looking for food and employment. In 1805 Joseph Gartside, who was employed by Greg, survived an attack in the woods by two men who fired pistols at him and stabbed him. Greg was offering a reward of twenty guineas for the successful conviction of the men. The crime wave became so severe that Greg paid £20 14s 0d for a group to prosecute felons in 1814. Twenty years later he was still employing 'watchers' to ensure the safety of his workers.

In around 1920, the Gregs introduced specially-bred pheasants into the woods for hunting parties. Beaters working on either side of the river with gamekeepers would disturb the pheasants, and Mr Gresty of Styal was on hand with his dogs to retrieve the fallen birds. The Gregs and other members of the gentry would sail up the river in a launch, polished and upholstered by the the Acton family.

Styal Methodist Chapel

The Chapel opened in 1833 in a former storehouse which belonged to Robert Hyde Greg, and is now owned by the National Trust. Alterations were made in 1858 to make it into a chapel and to extend its capacity. About three years later a vestibule was added and the frontage rebuilt.

Methodists in the area had been meeting together by 1784, sometimes in a cellar or renting cottages and farmhouses. In its early days, there was no permanent minister at the chapel and so visiting preachers came on the 'circuit horse' from Stockport. The minister would preach at Styal in the morning, then have lunch at Bank House Farm Oversley, where Methodists had met in earlier years, followed by a service in Wilmslow. He would return to Bank House where he stayed overnight before leading another service at Wilmslow on the Monday evening. The chapel was also used to teach elementary education in the evenings.

Thomas Waite was the local constable at Styal for nine years. He was the father of Terry Waite, the Archbishop's envoy who was held hostage in Lebanon for almost five years. PC Waite was noted for his unusual hobby of making dolls' houses. His work was displayed at the British Craftsmanship exhibition in 1951 and also seen at a London store. He was transferred to Lymm in 1953.

Terry Waite unveiled Styal Cross in its new location close to the old mill-workers' cottages and Norcliffe Chapel in 2010. It had previously been at the junction of Styal Road and Holts Lane until about 1860 when it was moved to the western end of Holly Lane. Although the base dates back to medieval times, the shaft and cross are more recent. It has since been restored and the cross was added by Robert Hyde Greg. A car badly damaged it in 1980, but following a campaign by the villagers it has been reconstructed with a piece of steel in the upright cross to keep it secure, at a cost of £7000.

Above: Oak Farm cottage is one of Styal's finest buildings. It is over four hundred years old and was owned by the Greg family before being given to the National Trust. It is part of a working farm and has been tenanted by the Gardiner family since 1884. Below: Cottages at Oak Farm, Styal.

Lode Hill

HENRY RUSSELL GREG

Henry Russell Greg (1832-1894) moved from Norcliffe Hall into the newly-built hall in about 1862. It was designed by JS Crowther, perhaps best known for his work on Manchester Cathedral, but also the architect of many country houses in the North West. Henry was the grandson of Samuel, the founder of Quarry Bank Mill, and the son of Robert Hyde. He was head of the family firm of H Greg and Co at Reddish cotton mills which employed about 400 workers, and was a director of the London and North-Western Railway Company. He was also President of the Manchester College which had its origins in Warrington before coming to Manchester in 1786, then moving to London and lastly Oxford.

His widow Emily was noted for her generosity towards good causes, and shortly before her death in 1914, she set up Lode Hill to become one of 2,787 registered War Hospital Supply Depots around the world. Volunteers supplied dressings and garments during WWI with flannel and wool provided by the Central Work Rooms, working to paper patterns to ensure efficiency and standardisation.

Manchester College, Oxford.

Walker family

Lode Hill

135

They made dressing gowns, pyjamas, operation gowns, night shirts, knitted woollen slippers, helmets, cardigans and socks. Bandages were made to the specifications of leading surgeons.

HENRY PHILIPS GREG

Henry Philips Greg

Henry Russell's son, Henry Philips (1865-1936), inherited his great-grandfather's commercial drive and greatly improved the business at Albert Mill, Reddish, Stockport. He was regarded as a good employer and one of the first to have a welfare officer to look after the health and well-being of the workers. A doctor and dentist regularly came to the mills, sports facilities were provided and evening courses organised. Greg was chairman of Ashton Brothers and the British Northrop Loom Company, and helped to establish the British Cotton Industry Research Association with laboratories at the Shirley Institute in Didsbury Manchester. The Greg family later donated land in Reddish for the building of a fire station, baths and library which were officially opened in 1908.

Like his father, Henry Philips was associated with the Manchester College, being its treasurer. He was also greatly interested in art and was treasurer of Whitworth Art Gallery and on the committee at

Lode Hill

Ship Inn, Styal.

Manchester Art Gallery. His wife Jennie had earlier studied painting in Florence. Their daughter, Barbara, left home at nineteen to study at the Slade School of Art between 1919 and 1922. At Lode Hill she had a studio where she worked on wood engravings which were commercially successful. She married fellow student Norman Janes, and they spent their life together as practising artists. Jennie Greg was a magistrate in Wilmslow and, like her husband, a staunch Liberal. She was a frequent speaker at their meetings and was an active campaigner on pensions and the plight of disabled prisoners. The Gregs were regular attenders at Norcliffe Chapel, Styal.

In the grounds of Lode Hill, Henry Philips had a model railway, which by 1933 could take up to five people along a 100ft-length of track. The locomotive was a scaled-down version of an existing steam engine with a tender for the coal and water. The engine and two trucks ran on bronze rails and gave rides for guests to the house at special events. He also helped the people of Styal by building a tea-room and setting up the Village Club at the time when Quarry Bank Mill was being run down. This was a popular venue for dances, plays and concerts.

He owned the Ship Inn at Styal, and because of problems with drunkenness set strict limits on how many drinks customers could have. They were allowed two drinks and would have to leave the bar for an hour before they could be served again. Greg was teetotal, and in 1919, he gave the adult males of Styal the option of converting the Ship Inn into a temperance establishment. As the nearest licensed pub was two miles away it is unsurprising that the locals voted for it to continue selling alcohol.

Lode Hill.

HENRY GAIR GREG

Henry (Harry) Gair Greg (1902-1978) inherited Lode Hill after his father's death in 1936, as well as being the main landowner in Styal. He lived there with his mother until WWII when the property was taken over by the RAF for training pilots, then later by the WAAF. Treasures from the house such as bronzes, china, paintings and silver were stored in the stables. After the War, because of the damage done to the house and problems with wood rot, Lode Hill was demolished and replaced with a bungalow. The family went to live at Oak Brow in the intervening period. The original wine cellar was incorporated into the bungalow and later, relatives were invited to take away its contents, but sadly it had become undrinkable. All that remains of the former house today are an archway with the Greg coat of arms and some of the old outbuildings.

Henry Gair was educated at Oxford and then worked at the family's mill in Stockport. He was a prominent figure in the industry and became chairman of the company, and involved with the Textile Institute. It is thought he ran the spinning section of the Reddish business at a loss rather than making the workers redundant. After his retirement from business he gave his time to preserving and developing the village, paying for a cricket pavilion and donating cricket and football

Quarry Bank Mill Archive, National Trust

138

pitches. He also inherited his father's passion for railways and had a workshop in the old stables where he kept the model steam engines.

Kath, the great-niece of Harry, remembers having rides with her brothers and sister and friends on the trains when she was little. There was a station with a canopy and two further stops with mini-platforms and roofs where there was a wind-up telephone to ring ahead of the train arriving. There were three carriages which carried up to four people on the line which arched in a semi-circular direction, going through the gardens and past the greenhouses. The engine would toot and whistle as it went on the five-minute journey. Kath recalled Harry as a kind and unassuming person. He was particularly proud of the peaches growing in the old walled garden from the days of the big house, and continued to employ gardeners to maintain the grounds and the vegetable patch. At his death in 1978 the villagers were given the opportunity to buy their rented property at a reduced rate.

Michael Janes, grandson of Henry and Jennie Greg, wrote about the family in 'From Smuggling to Cotton Kings'. His father

Henry Gair Greg outside the bungalow

Henry Gair Greg,
a benevolent employer
and landlord.

Quarry Bank Mill Archive, National Trust

remembered visiting Lode Hill with his parents in the 1930s and 1940s. Henry Philips and Jennie Greg lived on two floors and the servants on the top floor. A servant would come into his bedroom in the mornings and pull back the huge curtains on brass curtain rods. The house was filled with bronze statues and paintings. The painting 'The Blacksmith's Shop', painted by Joseph Wright of Derby in 1771, was later donated to Derby Museum in lieu of death duties in 1979. Jennie Greg would use the office in the mornings to order food and supplies for the household and these would be collected by the chauffeur. Two gardeners maintained the huge grounds with the miniature railway track and croquet lawn. Michael now has a big brass bed which came from Lode Hill after his parents were invited to choose some furniture from the old house. The grounds of Lode Hill are now used as parking for Manchester Airport.

Norcliffe Hall

The hall was built in 1831 for Robert Hyde Greg, then after his death it became the home of his second son Edward. Later, Ernest William Greg, Robert's grandson lived there until 1934.

Tom Barnes moved into the hall in 1938. He was company director of his family firm which manufactured ladies' aprons and overalls. He rented it until 1948 when the estate was purchased by the Higham family who had been living in Southport.

The hall was sold by the Highams in 1988 to be developed into a nursing home; however they retained the lodge. The hall is now private apartments.

Edward Hyde Greg's family: Front row L-R, Robert Philips, Madge, Helen, Alexander Carlton. Middle row L-R, Margaret Pearson, Beatrice, Edward Hyde, Margaret. Back row L-R, Robert Alexander, Mildred Alice, Edward Hyde Junior, John Tylston, Ernest William, Marian, and Thomas Tylston.

Robert Hyde Greg is believed to have built the Norcliffe stone circle after becoming interested in antiquities while travelling with his father on business trips around the world.

Memories of Styal and Oversley

Peter Scott who is now in his eighties, lived for 23 years in Styal. He was born and lived at Farm Fold, Styal in the row of cottages next to the Methodist Chapel. His family owned the Oversley Nurseries, Walter Scott and Sons, on Altrincham Road next to Oversley Lodge Farm. It was started by his grandfather and continued with his father and uncle. They specialised in growing dahlias and sweet peas, and exhibited in all the big flower shows such as Southport and Platt Fields Manchester. Walter came from Tarporley, and one of his first jobs was driving a steam engine from Quarry Bank Mill carrying cotton into Manchester. The nursery closed after Peter's father's sudden death.

Peter's grandparents lived opposite the nursery in a cottage. There used to be a wooden lintel over the door which stated that the bricks came from the demolished Knutsford Jail. There was a military firing range at the side of the nursery next to the River Bollin. After the War, military planes were scrapped and broken up here.

The old fire station was just to the side of the building next to the Ship Inn. There was a patch of grass with a bell on a post. The fire tender was pulled by a Humber car which was driven by Peter's father during the last War around Styal and Morley. The car was owned by Harry Greg who kept it behind the Inn. Peter played bowls and snooker in the building next to the pub.

Peter remembered the Gregs having an observatory at a farm on Moss Lane. This was destroyed in a gale. The Apprentice House at Quarry Bank became the home of the Estate Manager, Sammy Henshall, who lived there with his wife. An old lady used to live there on her own whom Peter used to visit. The downstairs was later used by Ready Radio to do repairs and then later by Reda's TV Repairs.

The old Styal post office was in the thatched cottages on Altrincham Road. The first cottage has two doors one of which led to the post office. Peter went on to work for the Bollin Valley Partnership supervising a youth employment team that felled trees, and built fences and bridges from Sutton to Warburton. There is a field off Moss Lane towards Oversley, near a wood close to the airport, where you could once see the ruins of 'Gresty', the game-keeper's cottage.

The old cottage, built with materials from the old Knutsford Jail.

Cottage door which once led to the village post office.

Oversley Brick Works

The works were started in about 1930 by Thomas Harrison who was born in 1873 and whose father and grandfather were Manchester brickmakers. His family and the Jacksons, another prominent Manchester family of brickmakers, merged in 1922 to form J&A Jackson Ltd. Thomas was the nephew of James Harrison whose seven sons all had connections to the business. The company eventually owned brickworks all across northwest England.

Thomas previously had a brickworks at Trafford Park on the site of the present Hay World Cargo company, between the railway line and the Bridgewater Canal. A tragedy occurred there in 1912 after a local six-year old boy got into difficulty when he slipped into a large fourteen foot deep clay pit belonging to the works. The boy's friends' cries for help were heard by Charles Thompson who worked at Harrisons and dived in to rescue him. Neither was seen alive again and Thompson was awarded a posthumous Carnegie Hero Fund medal for his bravery. The following year, Harrison was prosecuted for using a lorry and trailer filled with bricks which weighed more than the permitted twelve tons. The driver had ignored warnings not to go over the new Longford bridge which had to be re-paved after the incident, and Harrison was fined and had to pay costs.

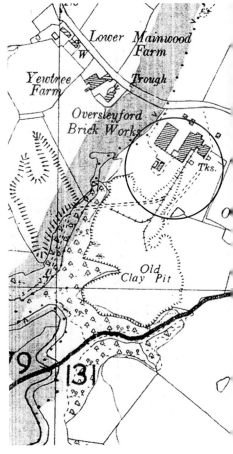

Harrison and his company, J & A Jackson of which he was chairman and joint managing director, purchased land at Oversley to replace other brickfields in the Manchester area. The company produced 200 million bricks a year which exhausted twenty acres of clay land annually. There had been considerable opposition to the establishment of the works because some thought it would cause industrialisation of the valley close to the Coward nature reserve at Cotterill Clough, Castle Mill outdoor pool and nearby residential areas. Jacksons argued that recent scientific developments ensured that there would be no black smoke emitted from the works, and that the new airport next to the site had already brought 'industrialisation' to the area.

The brickworks are to be seen with spectators' cars parked nearby.

In 1934 it was proposed that the works' chimney should be lit with neon lights and reduced by fifty feet to help the airport. Styal residents referred to the brickworks as 'Harrison's Pig', and all the locality would hear the lunch-time siren. During World War Two, when Ringway became a centre for training parachutists, the brickworks' chimney played an important role.

The proximity of the Bollin and a number of meres in the area meant that Ringway was susceptible to ground mists, which could delay training. Rather than wait for official weather reports, parachute instructors and pilots decided that if the chimney could be faintly seen from the hangars through the mist then the parachute jumps could go ahead. The chimney was also used for target practice with mortars and small weapons firing off blank ammunition. Joseph Harrison died in 1942 aged 69 in Sale where he had been resident for about twenty years. He was a keen crown green bowler and had followed the Manchester United team from its earliest days.

In 1958, Jacksons were amongst the objectors to the extension to the runway at Ringway Airport. They contended that future aircraft would not need long runways, and that the company's vehicles would be delayed whilst waiting for aircraft to taxi across the Wilmslow-Altrincham road. Jacksons also intended to excavate clay right up to the boundary by the end of the runway, although they had other land to work on before they got close to the airfield.

144

The former brickworks site in 1997 after it had been land-scaped and converted into an airport viewing area.

They were fined £50 in 1960 for dirty and inadequate first aid facilities. The company blamed employees who had not treated the facilities with due care. In November 1968 the problem of traffic holdups by aircraft going over the road to Wilmslow was solved with the opening of a four-hundred yard tunnel under the runway just to the south of the works and on the site of the old claypits. The tunnel, which replaced a nine hundred foot long section of the old road, had to be strengthened in mid-build to support the heavier and longer aircraft such as the Boeing 747 'Jumbo Jets' that would be using the runway. The tunnel cost £750,000 and took a year to build.

In the mid-1970s during a building recession, the company closed nine of the works including Oversley. The works lay derelict and after much discussion about whose responsibility it was, the brick-works' chimney was demolished on Sunday 29th June 1978. The airport was closed for five minutes after the explosion while a cloud of red dust dispersed. The demolition was executed by steeplejack John Derlin, who held a raffle to give the winner the opportunity to activate the explosives which would drop the 140-foot structure. Crowds blocked off lanes around the airport to watch the chimney crash down.

The former brickworks' site became a viewing area for the airport and was used by motorbike scramblers. Plans were submitted in 1983 for a nursery or garden centre there, with house and car park, but the site was later incorporated into land used for the Airport's second runway.

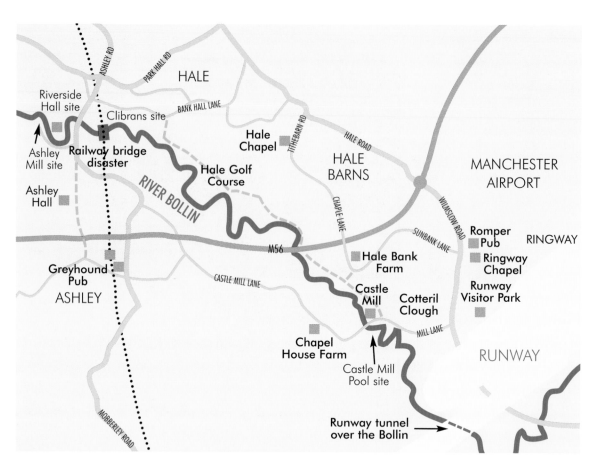

Riverside
Hall site

Ashley
Mill site

Clibrans site

**Railway bridge
disaster**

Ashley
Hall

RIVER BOLLIN

Hale Golf
Course

ASHLEY RD

PARK HALL RD

BANK HALL LANE

HALE

Hale
Chapel

TITHEBARN RD

HALE ROAD

HALE
BARNS

MANCHESTER
AIRPORT

CHAPLE LANE

M56

SUNBANK LANE

WILMSLOW ROAD

Greyhound
Pub

ASHLEY

CASTLE MILL LANE

Hale Bank
Farm

Castle
Mill

Cotteril
Clough

MILL LANE

Chapel
House Farm

Castle Mill
Pool site

Romper
Pub

RINGWAY

Ringway
Chapel

Runway
Visitor Park

RUNWAY

Runway tunnel
over the Bollin

MOBBERLEY ROAD

September 1998.

Len Grant

RINGWAY

146

September 1998.

Airport Runway Tunnel

Work began in the Autumn of 1997 on the R2 Project - the construction of a second runway at Manchester Airport, which would extend over the A538 Wilmslow Road, the River Bollin and into the countryside around Ashley, Mobberley, Wilmslow and Knutsford, at a total cost of about £190 million. It was the first full-length runway built at a major airport in the UK for over twenty years and was financed solely by Manchester Airport plc.

This was not the first time the airport had expanded into the Bollin Valley. By 1982 the first runway had been extended by 800 feet to 10,000 feet to enable bigger aircraft to come to Ringway. This required the river to be diverted with a newly-created embankment 360 feet long towering 82 feet from the valley floor. The embankment submerged most of Double Wood but naturalists were able to remove primroses and other plants before work began. The section which extended to the river was the world's first arrester bed or pull-up pad, filled with gravel and other materials which

June 1998.

A protester's hut on the Bollin in 1997.

would bring aircraft to a halt if they overshot the runway. The re-routed half-mile straight stretch of river needed a weir and stilling pond to slow the faster flow down. Nearly 100 acres of farm land were lost in the workings, but trees and shrubs were planted to help blend with the adjoining slopes.

The need for a second runway became apparent by 1991 to enable the airport to meet the growing demand for air travel in the region. The project was not welcomed by everyone in the locality nor by some environmentalists. Objectors claimed it would bring increased noise, pollution and environmental destruction. The airport and its supporters argued that the runway was vital for the region's economy and for future employment prospects. The National Trust was initially against the scheme but its opposition decreased after the airport handed over to them 100 acres of land around Quarry Bank Mill.

The bridging of the River Bollin was a particularly controversial aspect of the scheme, and airport planners had a boisterous meeting

A cliff by the Bollin in 1997 which was covered by the airport second runway.

Len Grant

Len Grant

lasting two hours with over 200 concerned people crammed into Ashley Village school hall. A public inquiry began in 1994 and lasted 101 days, recommending that permission should be granted in January 1997. Protesters against the second runway embedded themselves in six camps on sites around the runway boundary.

Above: The protesters were prepared to occupy the site for as long as possible. Their Christmas meal was reported to have been baked beans and mash. Below: Protestors set up a network of tree-houses.

The camps were named Flywood, Water/River Rat, Bollin Wood, Zion Tree, Wild Garlic and Sir Cliff Richard OBE Vegan Revolution. The protesters built tunnels, barricading themselves in, constructed tree-houses and chained themselves to trees. One man nailed his ear to a tree. Their efforts to publicise their cause and delay construction received much attention, especially when Daniel 'Swampy' Hooper joined the protesters. He was an experienced campaigner and had spent a record-breaking six days and twenty-three hours in the Big Mama tunnel during the A30 campaign in Devon. However, this record was beaten by four protesters in the Cakehole tunnel in the Bollin Valley Camp who were still vowing to stay there after seven days. One lady took eight weeks to dig a chamber she nicknamed the Moonshine Mine in the Flywood Camp, in which she spent 137 hours alone until bailiffs took nine hours to release her. Disco Dave

Len Grant

Top: A property being dismantled November 1997. Although there were fifty one listed buildings within a mile of the new runway, only four needed to be pulled down. The two timber-framed properties were reconstructed at Nether Alderley and Siddington in Macclesfield.

Above: Fragments of pottery discovered in 1978.

spent 156 hours in the Wormhole tunnel in the Sir Cliff Richard camp before he decided to give himself up. He had passed the time reading about the wartime exploits of the SAS.

By May of 1997 half of the camps had been cleared of protesters by bailiffs assisted by tree-climbers dressed in black and white. On 18th September 1998 permission was granted to evict the remaining protesters, watched by the world's media. The Under Sheriff of Cheshire was present as 200 security guards and 50 police officers carried out the evictions. However, a few days later, seven protesters managed to re-occupy the site until they were all finally removed the following month.

Work on site continued during the protest and the attempts to stop the felling of trees in Arthur's Wood. Limestone for R2 was brought from Derbyshire quarries by train via a specially constructed 1.3 mile spur onto the site which helped to remove an estimated 186,000 lorry journeys from the roads. Ancient woodlands, grass-lands and habitats were lost in the scheme, but in order to meet the many objections, £17 million was spent minimising the impact on the valley's natural and wildlife. An early Bronze Age settlement on the site was excavated, interpreted and recorded by archaeologists, and records and artefacts including flint arrowheads, pottery and tools handed over to Chester Museum. Some architecturally

June 1998.

September 1998.

Concorde takes off during tunnel construction.

151

Gavin Strang, the Minister of Transport, opens the railway link in December 1997 between the airport and Derbyshire quarries. Up to three daily trains delivered an estimated total of 1.3 million tonnes of limestone for the construction of the runway.

Len Grant

One of many new ponds created.

April 1999 - wildlife being collected and relocated to new habitats.

Len Grant

and historically important buildings were dismantled and either re-erected on other sites or put into storage. Wooden trackways were found by the Bollin which may have been used for fishing in the 18th century. Bat roost sites were dismantled and replaced with new boxes on the edge of the airport. Fish were removed to another part of the river during construction, 150,000 trees planted, 25 hectares of wildflower grassland created, and 97 ponds established or restored. Hedgerows were planted and new footpaths and bridleways created. Thirty four thousand newts, toads and frogs were collected by hand and taken to the new ponds. Rare mud snails were deposited at Chester Zoo. Plants and flowers including wild orchids were re-planted in new sites, and an artificial weir removed to allow fish to migrate up and downstream.

Those in charge of building R2 regarded the construction of the tunnel over the Bollin as the most complicated part of the scheme but also a key focal point. The huge structure would dominate this part of the valley, both from the noise of the aircraft and its intrusion on the natural landscape. Work began by moving 2.5 million cubic metres of earth to create an embankment to allow the new runway to cross the valley including the tunnel. The Bollin had to be temporarily diverted to enable work on the embankment and tunnel to proceed. Over thirteen months were spent building the 24 metres high embankment and the tunnel framework in all weather conditions, including the wettest summer for over twenty years in 1998. The single-arched tunnel of reinforced concrete required 2000 tonnes of steel reinforcement and 17,000 cubic metres of concrete. By July 1999 the work was in its final stages, with masonry cladding being added to the entrances, coping stones fitted into the river walls, and a public footpath laid as part of the Bollin Valley Way. The bat roosts and wagtail nesting boxes were already installed, along with the self-adjusting lighting which reflected ambient light conditions for the benefit of the ecology of the site. Contractors completed the R2 site by August 2000 when it was handed over to the airport.

Following a period of testing, the first commercial flight to use the runway was the Emirates Airbus A330-200 to Dubai on 5 February 2001. Emirates had outbid others for the honour of having the first take-off slot by donating £23,000 to children's charities. Passengers arriving at check-in for the seven-hour flight were invited to sign a commemorative book. At the departure gate they were served refreshments and received an engraved metal ticket as a memento of the occasion.

August 2000

August 2000

Spectators at what was originally known as Ringway Airport can watch the planes taking off from the Manchester Airport Runway Visitor Park. The Concorde Hangar and other aircraft exhibits are amongst the attractions here. Aircraft can also be seen from a raised viewing area alongside the runway near Altrincham Road Styal.

The Romper Inn and Ringway Chapel from Sunbank Lane.

Ringway Vicarage on the old Wilmslow Road.

RINGWAY

There has been a chapel here at Sunbank Lane since at least the 16th century. The Anglican church of St Mary's and All Saints was taken over during the Civil War by Nonconformists who resisted several attempts to remove them, until they left in about 1721 to meet in their own Unitarian chapel at Hale Barns which opened in 1723.

Ringway Chapel was rebuilt in 1723 and again in 1895. The wooden spire has been taken down because it was unsafe. The church remained in use until the declining population, due to the expansion of the airport, forced it to close in 1970. A new church has been built in Hale Barns. Ringway Chapel has been used by the Seventh Day Adventist Church since 2010.

ASHLEY & HALE

Hale Bank Farm

The front part was originally a farmhouse dating back to the late eighteenth century with a Victorian extension built onto the back. John Clarke, a land owner and surveyor, was living here in 1788 until his death in 1843. Richard Norton Scott, an ironmonger and merchant, resided there and died in 1857.

In May 1863 the grounds were used for a military fete, when NCOs of the 14th Hussars, then stationed in Manchester, celebrated the anniversary of a battle in India. The officers, their lady friends and the regimental band arrived in four omnibuses to enjoy a day of dancing and athletics. They returned to Manchester at sunset. The following year it was the scene of a tragic accident when the teenage son of the occupant, Hatton Elwin, a calico printer, accidently shot the young nursemaid. In 1862 Hatton had been discharged of business debts of £1794 by the Bankruptcy Court. He told the court that his problems in the cotton trade had been caused by the Civil War in America. He had previously had business premises at Fulshaw and Mosley Street Manchester. Prior to coming to Hale, he had been in Dartford, Kent.

James Kirtley was farming the 16 acres by 1851 and died in 1879. He was involved in a fatal shooting in 1858 while out with two farm labourers. As they were returning from a shoot, Kirkley's gun slipped to the ground and accidentally discharged into one of the labourers who died later at Manchester Royal Infirmary.

The farm was for sale in 1870 and again in 1880, with nine bedrooms, offices and 33 acres, and a quarter of a mile of good fishing in the River Bollin. David Madeley, a fustian manufacturer and merchant at China Lane Manchester, moved there in 1890 from Eccles, but died the following year. His wife Esther continued to live there.

Dr Douglas Moir and family came from Manchester to live here in about 1890. Moir, a homeopathic practiner born in Glamorgan, qualified at Aberdeen University. He was one of the founders of the Manchester Homeopathic Institution, Lower Byrom Street and had a daily surgery there. He attended Daniel Adamson, the pioneering engineer and one of the backers of the Manchester Ship Canal, in the last few weeks of his life in 1890. He was a churchwarden at Ringway Chapel for eighteen years, chairman of Ringway Parish Council and local overseer. His only recreation was gardening and he died while visiting one of his patients in 1924. His elder son was an anaesthetist at Manchester Royal Infirmary.

The property was later bought by Leslie Cussons, a member of the family who produced the Imperial Leather soap brand. During the last war, it had been requisitioned for the use of parachute packers and paratroopers. Some of those billeted there remembered the luxury of a private bathroom, a comfortable-sitting room and a tennis court. However, the old property was not treated well, and skirting boards were broken for firewood. The interior was later restored with the help of six prisoners of war who worked at the farm, and central heating was also installed. In the 1950s, the Cussons had a carved wooden bed brought from a Scottish castle. It was dated 1683 and reputedly slept in by Charles II and Nell Gwynn. Leslie Cussons died in 1963.

Above: Castle Mill by the Bollin.

Below: The Cheshire Yeomanry passing the mill. They became known as the Earl of Chester's in 1908, with 'A' Squadron having drill halls at Hale and Sale. They were the last regiment to fight on horseback, and later joined with the Welsh Border Mounted Brigade.

Chapel House Farm

The 58-acre farm at Thorns Green on Castle Mill Lane had become known as the Chapel House by the time of the 1871 Census. Tenant farmer William Overend lived there in about 1840 after moving from Stocking Heys Farm Mobberley. By 1851 William, then a widower, had moved to Blackshaw Heys Farm, Ashley with a son and daughter. Ten years later, the Overends were back at Thorns Green.

House which used to stand opposite Chapel House Farm.

The farm's later name of 'Chapel House' suggests links with the Nonconformist Church. All of William and Sarah Overend's twelve children were christened at Knowles Green Independent church at Pepper Street, Mobberley between 1814 and 1834, and the couple were married there in 1813. The old chapel had been built for the Wesleyans in 1783 (John Wesley preached here in 1785), but was taken over by the Independents in 1803, with chapel records up to 1837. Nearby is the recently closed Chapel House pub. The chapel was next used by the Congregational Church until its closure in the mid 1980s and is now a private residence. It seems possible that the Overends and others either transferred their services and fellowship meetings to Chapel House Farm after they left Mobberley or held additional gatherings there.

In about 1840, the farm was owned by William Dodge Cooper Cooper of Toddington Hall, Bedfordshire along with a further 225 plots of land he had inherited in Ashley, Timperley and Partington through his wife Elizabeth, the daughter of John Cooper of Bowdon. The farm later became part of Lord Egerton's Tatton estate.

By 1861, William Overend's son of the same name, had taken over

the running of the farm which he continued until his retirement, when it was taken over by his son Herbert. At the age of 75 in 1899, William was tragically killed after being struck by a train at Hale Station, then known as Peel Causeway. At the inquest into his death, the jury could not decide whether he had deliberately thrown himself in front of the train, and returned a verdict of 'accidental death'.

Hale Station

The farm was the scene of a murder in September 1894. There had been an argument between a number of Irish and English farm labourers returning on the 11pm train from Altrincham to Ashley. It escalated into violence with pitchforks taken from Chapel House Farm. During the fighting, which ended up in the farm granary, Thomas Meakin was stabbed in the lung and later died from his injuries.

During Herbert Overend's tenure of the farm, a Baptist Sunday School from Greenheys, Manchester spent the day there during Whit Week 1900. It was a regular practice for local farms to host Sunday School trips to the Bollin Valley. It was also a recommended stop for members of the Cyclists' Touring Club. The winged wheel CTC blue cast iron plaque on the wall of the farm (see the photograph on the opposite page) indicated to the weary cyclist they would find refreshments, showers, somewhere to hang or dry their clothes and have secure cycle parking. The club, founded in 1878, pioneered the endorsement of not only farms but also hotels and pubs which accommodated cyclists, as the leisure pursuit gained popularity in the late nineteenth century. Herbert died in 1926 and the farm has been in the occupation of the Erlam family to the present day.

Cyclists' Touring Club emblem

Above: Hale Golf Club which opened in 1903. The building to the left was known as The Cottage and was the home of the club professional until 1948, and then the club steward. The present club house was completed in 1996.

Below: The row of cottages c1906 which used to stand by the cross-roads opposite the Greyhound Inn at Ashley.

NH Spilsbury

Bridge collapse

In August 1860, during construction of the railway bridge over the Bollin near Bankhall Lane, the workings fell into the river completely blocking it up. Thirty men were working at the site but fortunately only four were on the bridge at the time. They were thrown over thirty feet with one of them sustaining serious injuries. The damage cost a few hundred pounds but work on the line was only slightly delayed.

Top: Clibran's who owned the nursery on Bankhall Lane were in Salford in the 1860s as a company making gas regulators. They became nurserymen at Partington and then Oldfield, Altrincham with the business rapidly expanding under Joseph Hargate Clibran by the 1890s. They gained a royal warrant, supplying seed for Hyde Park, trees for Sandringham and violas to Winston Churchill. They were also florists with a shop on Market Street Manchester. Nurseries were opened at Llandudno Junction, Bramhall, Urmston and Timperley. At its peak, Clibran's owned 400 acres and employed 400 people.

Above: Clibran's glass houses are to be seen beyond the field. The third generation of nurserymen, William Robert, died in 1964 and the nursery closed in 1968.

Riverside Hall was to the left
of the fence. Ashley Mill
is in the background.

John Henderson Brown

'The Bungalow' also know as 'Riverside Hall' at Ashley Heath, not far from Ashley Mill, was once the home of wealthy recluse John Henderson Brown. He was one of the biggest landowners in the district and yet people knew little about him. Neighbours sometimes referred to him as 'Bungalow Brown' (or Broun) and Altrincham was known as 'Broun Town'.

With the help of local architect and surveyor John Macnamara, he erected the Mossburn Buildings including the old post office buildings (1899) on Stamford New Road, Altrincham. The working relationship between Brown and Macnamara could not have been entirely harmonious because in 1900 the architect took him to court to successfully recover his fee of £1474 and £250 for libellous remarks made by Brown about his work.

Henderson next commissioned Station Buildings (1905) costing £40,000, now known as Stamford House, Altrincham's first office block. This went ahead despite several architects advising Brown against the project. It was designed by Manchester architect Charles Heathcote and built by George Grantham of Altrincham whose other work included the Unicorn Inn, Hale Barns and various local schools. Brown had a terrace of houses, 22 to 44 Willow Tree Road, Hale, built in the 1890s. He lived at 2 Queens Road, Hale before moving to his retirement home close to the River Bollin in 1896.

Three of John Henderson Brown's developments.

Top: Station Buildings

Middle: Mossburn Buildings

Left: Willow Tree Road, Hale

The Bungalow at Ashley Heath, which had unusually thick walls was hidden behind trees and designed in the distinctive terracotta style used for Station Buildings. There were impressive gardens and all the rooms in the house were finished in panelled oak, walnut and mahogany with oak parquet floors. The rooms were said to be plainly furnished with high-quality furniture.

Brown was born in Edinburgh in 1829, then moved to Broughty Ferry, a coastal suburb of Dundee. He came to Manchester and became wealthy through his dealings in the cotton trade, where he sold thread, and by selling his mill in Ancoats. Brown settled in Altrincham in about 1890 and used some of his fortune to develop parts of the town.

Henderson Brown never married, and had two domestic staff. He enjoyed long solitary walks around the Cheshire lanes on Sundays and made several much longer journeys on foot elsewhere. He reputedly walked three times to Edinburgh, the first as a tramp taking just a few shillings, to experience the feeling of poverty. He also frequently walked into Manchester, even though he had a season ticket for the train.

Above: A popular spot by the Bollin at Ashley Mill due to the generosity of Henderson Brown.

Below: John Henderson Brown plaque in the grounds of the former bungalow.

David Miller

Despite his eccentric behaviour, he was said to be amiable to all who approached him. He not only donated a strip of his land to widen Ashley Road between Hale Road and Bowdon, but also generously set aside a portion of his land by the River Bollin at Ashley Mill for the public to use, complete with seating, which proved extremely popular.

After a long active life, his health began to fail. The week before his death in 1910 at the age of 81, his doctor diagnosed he had heart problems and dropsy. One morning when the servant maid knocked on his bedroom door she failed to get an answer. It was Brown's habit to lock himself into his bedroom at night, and so the maid had to get help to force entry but he was found dead in his bed.

Ann Broun, thought to be John's neice, lived at Riverside until her death in 1925. It was later the home of Rev Cuthbert Ellidge Owtram who died in 1950. The bungalow was demolished in the late fifties but the owner of the new house on the site hopes to incorporate the John Henderson Brown plaque into the property.

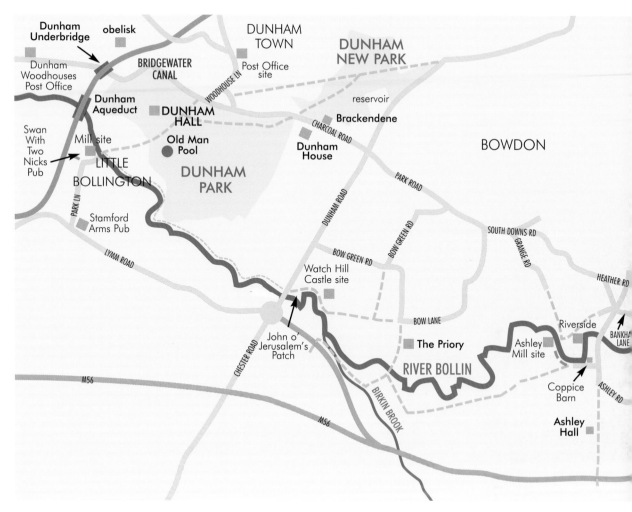

Woodhouse Lane, Dunham.

The Priory

A field archaeology survey undertaken by Manchester University in 2001 confirmed that the house stands on a raised area slightly higher than the lawns. There was evidence of an infilled mediaeval moat surrounding the 'island'. The dip in the lawn can just be seen in the above photograph.

The house had been Bowdon vicarage since the 13th century. In 1647 it was described as thatched, with three 'bayes', and a garden, barn and stables. A 1772 plan revealed it was also moated with nearby field names of 'Moat Croft' and 'Moat Brow'. There were about two hundred moated properties in Cheshire, and only four verifiable sites in Trafford. This moat is thought to have been a defence against feuding branches of the Mascy family. In about 1800 major changes to the building were made by the vicar, John Baldwin.

A new vicarage was built on Park Road in 1863 that befitted the increasingly prosperous neighbourhood, and the present building was bought by Josias Alexander. The house was re-named 'The Priory' (not to be confused with the Priory Hospital) in memory of its ancient links to the Birkenhead Priory. It contained thirteen bedrooms, a walled kitchen garden, and thirteen-acre grounds sloping down to the River Bollin. William Mackenzie, a coal shipping agent and landowner born in Edinburgh, lived here with his family until his death in 1897.

The Priory was purchased by George Inman and Ben Walmsley in 1899. Inman, whose grandfather was a surgeon, trained to be a doctor but never practised, although he used the title throughout his life. He helped to found the National St Bernard Club, and with Walmsley established kennels for breeding St Bernards at Barford near Bath. He was also a member of the Scottish Kennel Club. Walmsley, born in Bolton, was the director of a steel company and a pig iron consultant. By 1911 he had moved to Bowdon Old Hall.

The partnership continued at The Priory, and they were credited with producing the finest kennel of the breed ever seen. Their dogs had great success at shows and were continually in demand for stud purposes. It is claimed that all the best present-day St Bernards have descended from the Bowdon kennel. The partnership was dissolved in about 1903 and the kennel dispersed. Inman died in Japan in 1904. The following year, the house contents and farm stock and equipment were put up for sale.

Masonry from previous buildings on the site.

By 1907 The Priory was the home of Harry Gaddum, silk merchant, but best remembered for his philanthropic work. Born in Rusholme Manchester, educated in Switzerland, he went on to be the director of his father's company HT Gaddum and Co in Macclesfield. He was involved in various charities around Manchester including the City League of Health, the Boys' and Girls' Refuge Homes Association, and many other children's welfare organisations. He was chairman of St Anne's House Bowdon, a branch of the Manchester Ear Nose and Throat Hospital, and a magistrate

It is thought the moat followed the line of the existing ha-ha between the garden and a field to the east. A ditch to the west of the house may also have been part of the former moat.

Opposite: The Bollin near the Priory at Bowdon.

in Altrincham. Gaddum House on Queen Street Manchester, where many charities had offices, opened in 1936 and was named in his honour.

Manchester University awarded him an honorary degree in recognition of his work. After his death in 1940, his friend and co-worker Frank Dunkerley said that Harry Gaddum was the greatest optimist he had known. In response to social injustice Harry would admit it existed but go on to say 'Isn't it fun putting it right?' A plaque was unveiled at Gaddum House which read 'Harry Gaddum 1865-1940, A man greatly loved because greatly loving.' Gaddum House no longer exists but the service for disadvantaged people is continued at the Gaddum Centre, Jackson Street Manchester.

After the Gaddum family, the Priory became the home of the White family from 1959 for the next thirty years. At the time of purchase the Priory was in poor condition with dry rot and a tree growing in the lounge. The Gaddums sold the property relatively cheaply on condition the house's historic features were maintained. Tony Neary, the England rugby captain lived at the Well House.

Above and below: The Well House at the northern end of the Priory.

By the Bollin at Bowdon.

Representatives of Bollin Valley Partnership, Ramblers' Association and other local groups inspect the newly refurbished footpath by the Bollin at Bowdon which is part of the Bollin Valley Way, May 2016.

Brackendene

Katharine Septima Armitage aged 72, and four domestic servants moved into the house on Charcoal Road in 1901. She was the youngest daughter of Richard Hopper, a cotton and hosiery merchant in Nottingham. She described herself in the 1841 Census as 'a gentlewoman' inferring she was a person of high standing. Women of similar status would have subscribed to the Gentlewoman's Magazine, popular in eighteenth century England.

In 1871, at the age of forty-four, she married sixty-four year old Henry Oldland, a retired bookseller in Gloucestershire. He died nine years later leaving her the present-day equivalent of over two and a half million pounds. In 1890, she married seventy-four year old William Armitage JP, joint owner of the firm of cotton spinners Armitage and Rigby, with mills at Ancoats and Cockhedge, Warrington. His son, George Faulkner, was a notable architect and designer in the Arts and Crafts style, and mayor of Altrincham. After three years of marriage, William Armitage died in 1893, and Katharine lived at Townfield House Altrincham and then Langham Road, Bowdon before coming to Brackendene.

Above: Brackendene in 1982.
Below: Townfield House, Altrincham, previous home of Katharine Armitage before coming to live at Brackendene.

She was married for the third time in 1902 to Hume Nisbet, a novelist, poet and artist, whose wife had died the previous year. Nisbet was born in Stirling in 1849 and is remembered especially for his novels set in Australia where he had lived for seven years. He was a prolific author, completing forty novels between 1888 and 1905, four volumes of poetry, several short story collections, together with books on art and travel.

After returning from Australia he studied art in London, then went to Edinburgh where he became a theatre scene painter. He was an art teacher in Edinburgh for eight years as well as exhibiting at the Royal Scottish Academy. Afterwards he travelled through Australia, New Guinea, China and Japan producing articles and illustrations for the publishers Cassell and Co.

Hume Nisbet

Hume and Katherine stayed at Brackendene until 1904, then went to live at Beckington Abbey, Somerset. Katherine died in 1909 leaving an estate of almost £55,000, and bequeathed £10,000 to a rest home in Clifton, Bristol, £75 to animal charities, and £200 towards the maintenance of a clock presented by former husband Henry Oldland to a church in Stoke Bishop, Bristol. Hume married again in 1914 and died at his wife's home in Eastbourne in 1923.

Brackendene was advertised for sale in 1904, complete with stabling and six bedrooms, and set in over three acres. Calico printing business owner, Neville Assheton Clegg moved here with his family in about 1911. They gave permission for the house to be used by the British Red Cross for twenty wounded British and Belgian soldiers in 1914. Later the wounded were transferred to Raynor Croft, Altrincham. Clegg served on the advisory committees of Manchester Technical School and Manchester University School of Architecture and the management board of Manchester Royal Infirmary. The wounded were also treated at Altrincham Hospital, 'Heyesleigh' Timperley, Hale Congregational Church and Townfield House Altrincham.

The Cleggs remained at Brackendene until 1924 and the next year it became the home of George Hardy, managing director of the family-owned Hardy's Crown Brewery in Manchester. George and his wife Flora had been living at Pickering Lodge, Timperley, and when they moved, their head gardener, Derbyshire, came each day from Timperley to Dunham to maintain the grounds. The Hardys were listed there in 1939 along with George's sister Gladys and also in 1947. The house was for sale in 1956.

David George Pepler Norton, a liquidator occupied the house by 1967. His grandfather, George Pepler Norton, was a partner in the firm of accountants and liquidators Armitage and Norton in Huddersfield and around the country, and the author of 'Textile Manufacturers' Bookkeeping' published in 1889, which was regarded as a standard work on the subject for forty years. David's father, William Norton, was an engineer and joint MD of the firm Sir James Farmer, Norton and Co at the Adelphi Ironworks in Salford, and lived at Hollywood, Bowdon. David Norton and family were at Brackendene until about 1975.

Brakendene was then purchased for the use of the Iranian Consul. A former employee said that the house was well-maintained, and that many people attended parties there. The consulate office was at Booth Street from 1977, near Albert Square and by 1982 at 76 Princess Street. However, following the collapse of diplomatic relations between Britain and Iran in 1987 the five staff members including a vice consul were ordered to leave the country and the Manchester consulate was closed down.

Since then the house has badly deteriorated, suffering several arson attacks. Media organisations have published photographs of the poor state of the property since 2011. It remains in Iran's ownership and their officials have expressed their commitment to eventually restoring it. The gardens which continue to be maintained by local people, provide a spectacular display of daffodils in the Spring. It is to be hoped that this fine old property with its cultural, historic and international links can be saved in time.

Above: Brackendene today.
Below: The Bollin with the walls of Dunham Massey deer park in the background.

Dunham House

The mansion on Charcoal Road set in six and a half acres was built by 1901 for Edward Joynson JP, a retired Manchester textile merchant. It is of impressive design, featuring Ruabon mouldings. Joynson, born in Salford, had a silk and cotton business in Beswick, Manchester with his brother Peter, from which they retired in 1891. He also had a country home, The Glassert, at Aberfoyle, Scotland.

He was a Manchester magistrate for thirty years, and amongst his other interests he was one of the founders of Sale Public Library, patron of St Anne's church Sale, president of Sale Provident Society and member of the Sale Township Trust. He was also a supporter of the churches in Beswick, Manchester, a member of the Cheshire Hunt and trustee of the Manchester and Salford Bank. He lived at Ashfield Sale before moving to Dunham, but tragically it was for a short time. His wife was in poor health and in 1904 whilst on holiday to Corfu, he contracted pneumonia. His own doctor was brought over from England but could not save him. Mrs Dorothy Joynson died ten months later in Conway.

The sixteen-bedroomed mansion was put up for auction in 1906 but seems to have remained unoccupied until 1909 when John Sington and family moved there from Whalley Range, Manchester.

St Philip's, Bradford Road Manchester, known as the 'Joynson Memorial'.

He worked in his father's company at Princess Street, Manchester which imported and exported textile machinery. He became Deputy Lieutenant of Lancashire and was a Major in the Royal Engineers. Sington appears to have converted from Judaism to Christianity in order to marry Mildred Maclure whose uncle was the Anglican Dean of Manchester.

Both his sons were army captains who survived the First World War, and so he set up a fund as a 'Thanksgiving Offering for their safe return'. Known as the 'John Sington Fund' it provided help for the dependants of servicemen from Bowdon or Dunham Town who had been killed or disabled. John Sington provided a further £1000 to the fund in his will at his death in 1922. The fund continued to support many people until 2008 when it was removed from the Charities List. The stories of the claimants are to be found in the Minutes Book now kept in Trafford Local Studies Library.

After the First World War, John's sons, Edward and Alan became barristers. During the Second World War, Edward re-enlisted and successfully led his men through France to evacuation at Dunkirk. John's great-nephew, Derrick Singleton, was the first British officer to enter the Belsen concentration camp and announce the Allies had arrived. He later gave evidence at the Nuremberg trials and married a Belsen survivor.

Below: Ruabon mouldings around the windows.

By the time of the last war Alan Sington, who lived at Dunham House, was one of the country's foremost Alsatian trainers and won many awards at dog shows. Hundreds of dogs belonging to servicemen were kept in the kennels at Dunham House. The specially heated kennels housed locals' dogs while they were away on holiday and evacuee dogs from around the country, including a spaniel which had been sent from London after its master's home had been destroyed by enemy bombs. Mona Griffiths, once one of the King's veterinary surgeons and an expert on Alsatians, was the chief kennel manageress and lived at the lodge.

Dunham House was commandeered in 1941 to become a special centre for training parachutists.

Major JC Edwards was the Commandant here throughout the Second World War and the instructors were mainly British Army officers. In this secluded location they trained by dropping through a hole in the floor of a replica of the fuselage of a Whitley bomber. It was a rather tight fit getting through the space and many experienced knocks to their faces, especially the nose, which was nicknamed 'ringing the bell' or 'the Whitley kiss'.

The gates to the house were guarded because many of the parachute students were training to be S.O.E. secret agents, including the now-famous Odette Hallowes whose experiences were made into a feature film; an agent, code named 'White Rabbit', who has been likened to James Bond, and Peter Churchill who infiltrated into France by both submarine and parachute. However one student was arrested there on suspicion of being a Nazi sympathiser.

A group of the agents used to enjoy a drink at the Stamford Arms but were under strict orders not to divulge anything about their activities. Dunham House was the venue for training, code-named 'Jedburgh', with teams consisting of different nationalities who were to be parachuted close to the enemy front line to support resistance forces. Another programme run at the house known as the 'Bonzo scheme', trained anti-Nazi German prisoners of war. York House, Timperley and Fulshaw Hall, Wilmslow were also used for this purpose. Some of the instructors took part in a night drop over Dunham House, and embarrassingly one of them became entangled in one of the roof turrets and had to be released with much merriment by the ladies of the Auxiliary Nursing Yeomanry who were employed there as administrative staff and lived at the lodge. Alan Sington died in 1948, and Dunham House has been converted into private apartments.

There has been a shop here at Dunham Town since 1850 then run by Sarah Dean. In 1897, Emma, the widow of grocer Samuel Clarke, became the first sub-postmistress. By the time of her death in 1920, she had worked at the shop for fifty years.

In the 1930s there was a public phone inside the post office with a bell-shaped ear-piece and separate mouthpiece. To make a call, a handle had to be wound up. Later a phone box was installed, which was eventually moved to its present position. The post office closed in 2008, with Joan Pendlebury becoming its final postmistress although the shop is still open.

Chris Hill

DUNHAM

The post office at Dunham Woodhouses has been run by three generations of the Wareham family since about 1888. Frank was listed there in 1901 as a grocer and market gardener, then in 1906 as also sub-postmaster. Previously he had been a gamekeeper. He and his wife had run the business for over thirty years until his death in 1919.

It was taken over by his son Frank William who died in 1932 and had been the sub-postmaster for thirteen years. He was a member of the village prize band, and had been its honorary treasurer. He was

also a member of the local golf club and attended the Primitive Methodist Church in the village. Before taking over the post office, he had been a shopkeeper and poultry dealer on Church Street Altrincham.

His son, Frank Harold, was the sub-postmaster at the time of his wife's death in 1953. Like his father he was also a gardener. He died in 1972 and the post office closed the following year. It had re-opened by 1976 for a further two years.

POW camp, Dunham New Park

The New Park to the north-east of the old Park was in existence by 1702 on farm land. It was first known as High Park and reputedly designed by Capability Brown. A walkway through the park to St Mary's Church Bowdon was made, and a building, 'The Seat', erected at the eastern end on high ground with views over the park.

The Boy Scouts were granted permission for a permanent camp in the area of the park known as Home Park in 1921. Chief Scout Lord Baden Powell attended a reunion in 1932 of Scout masters who had been trained there during the past ten years. The New Park area was requisitioned by the War Department in 1942 for the use of American troops, who arrived the following year. They were housed in two separate camps - North and South.

After the troops moved out in May 1944 in readiness for the Normandy Invasion, it became a prisoner of war camp for 3500 Germans which later rose to 6000. Trees were felled and an extra perimeter fence constructed with two watch towers. Germans of all ranks were sent from other camps and guarded by the Free Polish Army who patrolled the perimeter fence. British troops were only involved in administrative duties. This was one of twenty PoW camps in Cheshire. No-one ever escaped from the Dunham camp, where they were interrogated, searched regularly and counted several times daily. The prisoners all had shaven heads and highly polished boots. The SS troop contingent, known as 'Rommel's Men' had their blood group tattooed on their arms. Italian PoWs were also kept there, but they were kept separate from the Germans because of their mutual hatred. They always wore brown shirts and ties. Local girls used to pass on chocolates and cigarettes at the perimeter fence, and people remember the massed ranks of Italians marching to St Vincent's RC Church on Sundays.

The POWs were housed in 220 concrete, timber or corrugated huts on the site. Initially the POWs received sparse rations but gradually conditions improved. Prisoners laid lawns and flower beds around the huts, and also constructed a football pitch with terraces. Regular church services were held there, and a theatre, built by the American troops, was used by the POWs to put on concerts with choirs and an orchestra. They also spent their confinement making craft items and attending classes in languages, business studies and

A 1939 gathering of 2000 Lancashire Boy Scouts at Dunham had a surprise visit from the Crown Prince of Abyssinia accompanied by Lord Stamford and the northern Chief Scout.

other subjects. Some of the prisoners were allowed out to work in nearby farms and on the Dunham estate. Many of them established friendships with local people, and some of them married local girls and settled in the district. One became the manager of the Grapes pub on Regent Road, Altrincham. Another was the groundsman at Timperley Cricket Club while others worked at Clibran's Nursery Hale and on the Manchester Airport runway extension. Towards the end of the war, restrictions within the camp were lifted, the perimeter guards were withdrawn and the public were allowed in.

A model of a Bavarian castle opposite the entrance to Denzell made by the prisoners out of scrap material used to be popular with Sunday visitors. It was later broken up and used in a garden rockery in Oldfield Brow. Bert Trautman, the famous Manchester City goalkeeper, himself a PoW elsewhere, took part in a football match at Dunham between former prisoners and a Manchester team at the end of the war.

In December 1946 the PoW Camp re-opened as a temporary depot for the Manchester Regiment and for use as the 63rd Primary Training Centre for National Service recruits. The interiors of the huts had been repainted in green and cream by a hundred former prisoners. A wall was built in the middle of each hut with fireplaces replacing the original stoves. Each recruit would be allowed five days' leave at Christmas and a weekend off after four weeks. Although lights out was at 10.30pm, recruits could stay out longer with permission.

There was great pressure for the military to leave the park and in 1947 a deputation of councillors from Altrincham and Bucklow was assured by the War Office that they were looking for alternative sites. However in May 1948 the camp was still in use, and there was a visit from HM the Queen to a military parade where a Military Cross was awarded. This was the Sovereign's first public duty as Commander-in-Chief of the armed forces. Troops finally left the camp in November 1948 with the proviso from Mr Shinwell, Secretary of State for War, that the North camp should be handed back if war threatened.

Local councils hoped to use the old camp huts for housing following the post-war shortage, although it had been agreed with Lord Stamford that the park should eventually

Huts from the former PoW camp were re-erected at Lark Hill Timperley in 1950 for use as a meeting place. The old Red Cross hut was demolished in 1999 and replaced the following year by the Larkhill Centre and officially opened by Lady Ashbrook.

Hazel Pryor

become a public park. Since the 1880s, there had been suggestions that Dunham Hall and its parks and forest should become the 'Hampton Court' or 'Epping Forest' of the north for the people of Manchester. The writer of 'Manchester Faces and Places' described the New Park as 'the most beautiful bit of forest scenery near Manchester'.

In 1959 the New Park was leased from Lord Stamford by a group of Manchester businessmen to form the Dunham Forest Golf Club. 'Tirbracken', the former home of the late Judge Hogg, was planned as the clubhouse. The house had dry rot and, following a fire, it was demolished and a new clubhouse built on the site. Thousands of tons of timber had to be felled and great quantities of fern and birch saplings uprooted, although the wooded aspect of the course was retained. 40,000 tons of concrete from the old camp were also removed. The nine-hole course opened in 1961 and was expanded to eighteen in the mid-1970s after more land was acquired. The course is regarded as one of the most scenic in Cheshire. Most of the surviving huts from the old military and PoW camp were demolished for the building of a covered reservoir holding 24 million gallons. It suffered a serious fire in the control room within four days of opening in November 1965.

Above: The remains of the foundations of several huts from the camp are to be found amongst the trees by the golf course.

Below: Dunham Forest Golf Club, with the embankment of the reservoir in the background.

Stamford Hospital
Dunham Hall

It was one of nearly 3,300 auxiliary hospitals opened in the First World War to deal with the thousands of casualties. 282 servicemen were treated here, with only one death recorded. During WWI this and twelve other sites in the Altrincham area were taken over by the Red Cross and Order of St John and known as VADs - Voluntary Aid Detachments.

Roger Grey, the 10th Earl of Stamford, was away on war duty in London, and so the commandant of the hospital was the Countess Penelope Grey, with Lady Jane Grey, the earl's younger sister, a VAD nurse here. The medical team was led by Sister Catherine Bennett who was noted for her one-to-one care when treating aneurysms, and continued to work tirelessly and beyond the call of duty until the end of the war. When the hospital closed she went to the Balkans, where she worked at a Serbian Relief Fund Hospital. A framed letter from the War Office hangs at the hall, thanking the staff at the hospital for the wholehearted attention they gave to the patients in their care.

The Perkins family were amongst the volunteers at the hospital. Algernon Edward Perkins was the Hon Secretary, Treasurer and Quartermaster at Dunham. His family were owners of a brewery in Shropshire and he inherited a substantial income from it.

Above: The nursing staff receiving awards. They had ever-increasing numbers of patients after starting with 25 beds. The nurses worked 12-hour shifts treating a wide range of medical conditions.
Below: Patients were encouraged to spend time in the gardens to aid their recovery.

He and his wife Meriel Gundreda Leighton lived at Sundorne Castle near Shrewsbury for about ten years until 1905. Just before the outbreak of war, brewery shares tumbled and Algernon's £12,000 a year income dwindled to virtually nothing and he was declared bankrupt.

Meriel Perkins was the daughter of Lady Leighton Warren of Tabley House, Knutsford who was married to Sir Baldwyn Leighton, Bart, of Loton Park Shrewsbury and presumably had a private income. When Meriel's mother died in 1915, she bequeathed her a large solitaire diamond ring given by the Empress of Russia, to the family.

Cynthia Perkins

At the outbreak of war, the Perkins with their daughters Meriel Elizabeth and Cynthia Gundreda, came to live at Hempfield, Dunham Town. Before they commenced at Stamford Hospital, Meriel Gundreda was nursing at the 2nd Great Western Hospital in Manchester which had its HQ at Whitworth Street School and other branches around the City. Her daughters first nursed at Haigh Lawn, Altrincham then Meriel moved to Dunham in 1916. In 1918 both sisters had measles and their mother took time off to look after them.

Meriel Elizabeth Perkins

Meriel and her mother were commended for their work in a list sent by the Red Cross to the Secretary of War in 1919. Meriel Elizabeth is seen in a photograph at Dunham with a doctor and Sister Bennett dressed for surgery. Meriel was mentioned by the Countess in a letter as being 'very useful and helpful'. After the War, Algernon and Meriel remained at Dunham Town until about 1921. Meriel and her daughters are in the 1920 photograph of the Dunham Massey WI, hanging in the village hall. Algernon and Meriel went to live at Bexhill-on-Sea, Kent. Algernon died in 1926 and Meriel Gundreda at Cardiston Manor near Shrewsbury, in 1947.

Meriel Elizabeth travelled to Canada in 1926 and in 1935 broke off her engagement to the Rev. Arthur Walker of Birmingham after one month. She went to New Zealand in 1953 and died in England in 1967. Her sister Cynthia married the Rev. Charles Williams DSO in 1932.

The Countess (left) and Meriel Gundreda Perkins (middle right).

Old Man Pool

Old Man Pool, Dunham Massey was at the centre of a curious tale about a pike seen in the pool one evening by a Dr Warwick in 1869. He noticed that as it darted away it struck its head on a hook which was fastened to a post. The small pike then swam rapidly backwards before diving to the bottom of the pool and then throwing itself onto the bank. The doctor picked it up and found that the hook had pierced its skull.

He managed to press the brain into the correct position with the aid of a silver toothpick. The fish remained still while the doctor treated it. He then returned it to the water, but the pike seemed agitated and repeatedly threw itself out of the pool. With the help of a gamekeeper he constructed a cradle in which the fish could lie.

The following morning the doctor came back to the pool and the pike swam to the edge and rested its jaw on his boot, and allowed him to check the wound. As Dr Warwick walked backwards and forwards along the edge of the pool, the pike followed him. However when it could not see him on its injured side it became agitated. From then onwards, whenever he visited the pond, the pike would either be waiting for him or respond to his whistle.

The doctor brought his family and friends to feed the pike but it reserved its attention for him. Sadly it was later shot by a relation of the Earl of Stamford who was unaware of the pike's unusual behaviour.

It was at this pool in August 1907 that William Grey, the ninth Earl of Stamford, while out walking with his two young children, his wife and Lord Grey of Groby, suffered an attack of 'giddiness' and fell into the water. He recovered quickly and was able to complete the walk.

William Grey, the ninth Earl of Stamford.

183

The sundial-bearing figure was one of 18 statues and monuments installed during the landscaping and replanting of the park by the second Earl of Warrington.

The sandstone obelisk on the edge of Whiteoaks Wood by the Bridgewater Canal marks the northern vista from Dunham Hall. It is an 'eye-catcher' which was sited at the end of a tree-lined avenue now split by the canal completed in 1765. This and a similar obelisk at Langham Grove are thought to have been built in about 1714 by Thomas Grey the 2nd Earl of Stamford who was known for recklessly spending his inheritance.

There is a tradition that a racehorse which recovered the fortune of one of the Earls of Warrington was buried here. George Harry Grey, the seventh Earl spent many thousands of pounds on racing. Two of his horses won the Two Thousand Guineas race at Newmarket and another came first in the Oaks at Epsom Downs.

185

Dunham Underbridge

The bridge which carries the Bridgewater Canal over Woodhouse Lane used to be a stopping-off point for passengers to Dunham Massey. In the 1850s they sailed from Knott Mill Manchester for the return fare of 6d. Maps in the 1870s and 90s refer to the bridge as the 'Woodhouse Lane aqueduct'.

The low bridge, combined with the bend and dip of the road, have been the cause of several notable accidents. In 1871 some of a party of thirty-four teachers and singers from Great Lever Church Bolton were badly injured when their omnibus hit the masonry. Afterwards they were taken to the Griffin Inn at Bowdon for medical attention. In about 1873 a well-known Irish comedian of the time was killed here when a coach collided with the bridge.

Then, in 1889, a party from Salford on their way to a picnic at the Rope and Anchor pub in a long coach pulled by five horses came into difficulty under the bridge. As the coach driver approached the bridge he realised there could be problems and requested the passengers get off before they entered the bridge. Although some did as they were requested, the majority decided it was safe and remained on board and told the driver to keep going. James Beckett had foolishly climbed onto the roof of the coach to gauge the space. Tragically, the coach roof and canal bridge came into contact and he died from his injuries soon afterwards, while three others were treated for minor knocks.

At the inquest held at the Rope and Anchor, a witness stated that on the journey the coach already had brake problems, which had been repaired with old shoes. The deceased, a 33-year old railway clerk, had shouted to the driver that there was plenty of room. The police confirmed that the bridge had been the site of many accidents and requested that the coroner contact the Manchester Ship Canal Company to put warning notices on the bridge.

The bridge caused problems for the North Western buses which ran from Altrincham to Lymm and Warrington. In 1964 ten custom-built low-chassis vehicles with flat roofs were ordered, to contend with the bridge. The buses had been designed for use in South America. The bridge had to be closed in 1971 following a breach in the canal. The present bridge, made of concrete and metal, has a trough which carries the water across, and took over two years to complete.

Above: The rebuilt bridge today with its height clearly shown. Below: The Rope and Anchor, where the 1889 inquest took place.

187

LITTLE BOLLINGTON

Top: The Stamford Arms c1905 just before Thomas Webster, who was managing the Swan, took over. Above: The Swan With Two Nicks.

Opposite: (Right) John Davenport, miller at Little Bollington. His father, James, was previously miller at Castle Mill and Ashley Mill. James's father-in-law James had been a special constable on duty at the Peterloo Massacre. (Left) John's son of the same name who lived at the Mill House by the Bollin before moving to Slaithwaite in Yorkshire in about 1884. (Middle) John's son - John Shaw whose daughter Marjorie was a teacher at Altrincham Girls' Grammar School.

Jean Peters

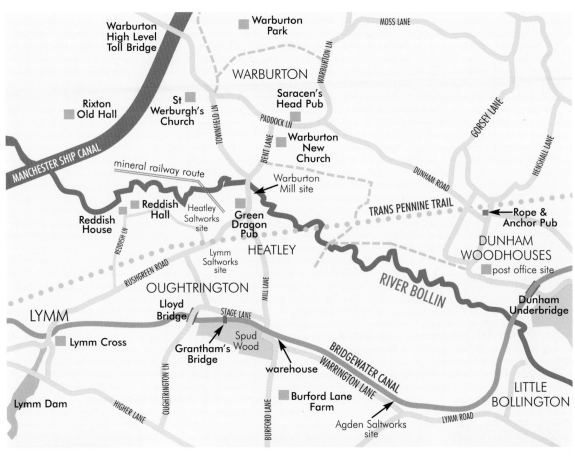

*The Burford Lane warehouse on the Bridgewater Canal at Oughtrington
began as a hospital for horses being used on the canal.*

NH Spilsbury

Remains of the track no longer visible on the trail route.

NH Spilsbury

The track being lifted from the Warrington-Timperley section of the railway at Sinderland Crossing 1988.

The Trans-Pennine Trail follows part of the old Warrington-Stockport railway, between Broadheath and Lymm.

Left: Plaque mounted on a stone by the trail near the Rope and Anchor pub celebrating forty years of the Bollin Valley Partnership.

Below: The former Dunham Massey station buildings which are now a private residence beside the Trail.

The station then known as 'Warburton Station' opened on the Warrington-Stockport line in 1854. It was re-named 'Warburton and Dunham' in 1856, and finally 'Dunham Massey' in 1861 until its closure for passenger traffic in 1962. Freight trains continued to use the line until 1985. In this photograph from 1947, the Rope and Anchor pub is to the left. Warburton bridge is just beyond the station.

Burford Lane Farm

Designed by architect John Douglas in 1866 for George Charnley Dewhurst, an East India merchant, cotton spinner and manufacturer, and head of the firm G and R Dewhurst, commission merchants and shippers, Gt Marlborough Street, Manchester. Dewhurst, who purchased many properties in the district, owned 1549 acres by1873. Dewhurst lived at 'Beechwood' formerly the home of local solicitor Thomas Ridgway. All that remains of the estate today is the old stable block, now the changing rooms of Lymm Rugby Club, and an arch on Crouchley Lane. Dewhurst later bought a home in the Perthshire Highlands where he spent most of his time and died there in 1894. Both George and successive generations were prominent in the life of Lymm until 1911 when their Beechwood and Oughtrington properties were sold.

The Grade II-listed farm with 107 acres on Burford Lane is thought to be one of Douglas's earliest farmhouses in the Arts and Crafts style. His work is to be seen throughout the North-West and parts of Wales. He was responsible for the Grosvenor Hotel, the City Baths in Chester and also the iconic Eastgate Clock, one of the most photographed time-pieces in Britain. The City Council weren't convinced about its design and only half of the members came to the opening ceremony in 1899. He also designed housing at Port Sunlight and was principal architect to the Duke of Westminster.

Douglas lived at 'Walmoor Hill' on the banks of the Dee in Chester, in grounds which included trees brought from around the world.

Eastgate clock Chester, designed by John Douglas. There are many examples of his work in Warburton.

He outlived his wife and four of his five children. The fifth, Sholto, although encouraged to become an architect, lived a life in complete contrast to his hard-working churchman father. Sholto never worked, preferring to spend lavishly and drink heavily. John Douglas was also architect to the Duke of Buccleuch and Queensferry and tragically died while at Dumfriesshire in 1853. The horse-drawn gig in which he was travelling overturned and he was dragged along in it for twenty yards before being thrown out.

Below: Grantham's Bridge at Oughtrington built by James Brindley c1770.

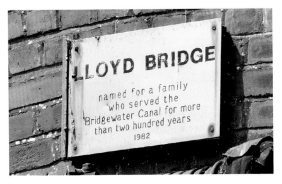

Above: The bridge on the Bridgewater Canal at Oughtrington was built by James Brindley in about 1770. It was re-named Lloyd Bridge in 1982 following the retirement of Thomas Lloyd, a canal and river inspector from the Manchester Ship Canal Company. He was the last of eight generations of his family to work on the canals. His ancestor, John Lloyd, a boat-builder from Bangor-on-Dee, helped the famous engineer, James Brindley, to build the Bridgewater Canal. Thomas began working for the Ship Canal Company in 1933 as a 'brew lad' and later became responsible for the maintenance of the whole fifty miles of waterway.

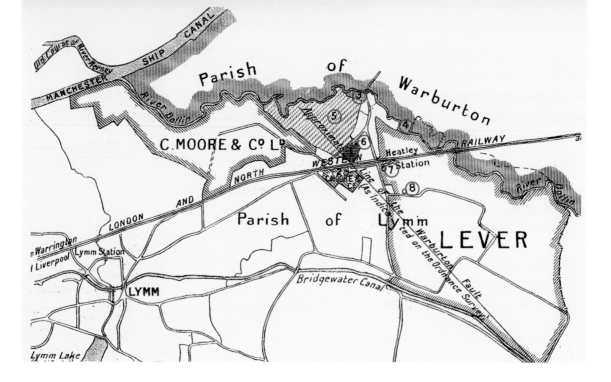

Lymm Salt Works

In about 1900 it was established that there was an area of high-quality brine located close to the Stockport-Warrington Railway and the Manchester Ship Canal at Heatley, south of the River Bollin. Edward Allen of Bowdon, a mining engineer, instigated the exploratory work with test borings, pretending to be searching for coal. He then bought parcels of land or mineral rights to sell on to salt companies. There were proposals to lease land by the canal to salt manufacturers for export.

The effluent from one of the boreholes flowed into a brook at one of the neighbouring farms. A farmer's wife could not understand why her ducks would not go into the brook as they usually did. In exasperation she took a duck by the neck and held it in the stream. But then the sting from an open cut on her hand from the salt convinced her that the water was no longer pure.

Soap makers Lever Brothers of Port Sunlight, also bought 1340 acres of the Heatley portion of the Dewhurst estates in 1911 to begin production. This included the properties of Oughtrington Hall and House, Beechwood Hall, and Lymm Dam. William Lever planned to incorporate the village of Lymm into a garden city, and began work on an estate for his workers. However, because of an agreement with commercial rivals, he did not proceed with a salt works.

The works owned by Charles Moore and Company and known as Lymm Salt Works opened in about 1905 where they produced 'Lymm Pure Salt'. This was made possible through a patented process of evaporation which made 99.98% sodium chloride. The brine was pumped 400ft from twelve boreholes to the south of the works, which continued production twenty-four hours a day, seven days a week. It was transported by train in distinctive house-shaped red vans. Each of the three shifts to produce fifty tons of salt daily began with the sound of a steam hooter. During the last War, the hooter was used as an air-raid siren.

The works were on the 'Warburton Fault', and the main 120ft-high brick chimney could be seen from miles away. The works were subject to many local complaints about the smoke and offensive smells. Despite the rich reserves of brine, they closed in about 1951, due to problems with spreading subsidence close to residential property.

Former route of the planned saltworks railway at Heatley.

Heatley Works

A second salt works were built by JJ Verdin Cooke of Liverpool to the south of the River Bollin at Heatley after brine of excellent purity was found there. Heatley Salt Works opened about 1914 on a 23-acre site, with a concrete bridge built over the Bollin to provide a rail link to the works from the main railway. The company had hoped to transport the salt on the nearby Ship Canal but the shortage of shipping at the outbreak of WWI prevented it. They had also secured the rights to lay a pipe from the works to the canal. The company closed the business in 1925 after difficulties with high local rates and Lymm UDC's refusal for expansion.

Agden Works

Agden Salt Works opened in 1922 beside the Bridgewater Canal. These were much smaller than the other two works, specialising in salt for the food and curing industries. They closed in 1959 and some of the buildings were used as a boat yard. The old Lymm works site is now a residential estate, and the remains of the Heatley works were cleared many years ago. The long straight route of the proposed works railway, remains to the north of the Bollin.

Lymm Historic Transport Festival 2016.

Above: The former Lymm Parochial School, which opened in 1863, can be seen behind Lymm Cross c1950. It was known as Pepper Street Junior School before demolition was completed in 1969.

The origins of Lymm Cross are uncertain but the cross and steps were restored for Queen Victoria's Jubilee in 1897. The Cross has long been a focal point of the village and is set on an outcrop of red sandstone. There are three sundials with the inscriptions; 'Save Time', 'We are a Shadow' and 'Think of the Last'. In the cottages opposite the Cross, there used to be Ivy Flanagan's chip shop on the left, and a dentist's surgery to the right. Beyond the cottages was the Co-op store.

Reddish Hall

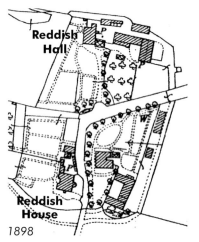

Reddish Hall

Reddish House

1898

Several generations of the Grundy family lived both at Reddish Hall in this large property with nine bedrooms and four entertaining rooms, and at Reddish House. By 1861 Margaret, the widow of Thomas a surgeon was at Reddish Hall with her two sons; Edward, who took over the farming of the 80-acre estate, and Thomas, the head of the firm of Manchester solicitors Grundy Kershaw and Co. Some of the field names on the 16 acre property which went down to the River Bollin were linked to the legal profession such as 'The Barrister' and 'The Magistrate'.

In 1881 it was occupied by John Pattenberg a commission agent and chemical merchant. He went to live in Scotland and died there in 1892. Donald Macpherson, a paint, varnish and Chinese lacquer manufacturer, was at the hall in 1891. He founded his company in Manchester in 1884 and it expanded to become the fourth-largest coatings company in the UK by the 1980s. They supplied paint to Woolworths, who sold it under the 'Household' own-brand label, before the company was acquired by Crown Paints in 2008.

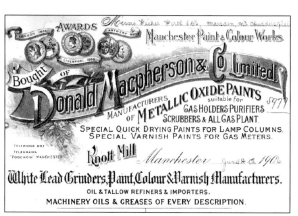

1906 Macpherson's billhead. They were at Knott Mill Manchester, with works at London, Liverpool and Anterp.

James Hatton Hall (1866-1945), a merchant with business premises in Manchester, London and Calcutta, lived here in 1901. He was the son of a Chorley victualler and lived for a short period at 'The Willows' Timperley (the author's home) in around 1894, before moving to Hale. Hall became a pioneer of the rubber industry in British North Borneo and Brunei.

Reddish House

This was the home of Thomas Grundy surgeon, at the time of his death in 1814. The house had been recently built and consisted of six bedrooms and three parlours. Outside there was a garden stocked with fruit trees and fields extending over two Cheshire acres. After his death the house was to let, and his apothecary's drugs were sold. The Grundy family were substantial landowners in the district with around 130 properties when the tithe maps were compiled. Grundy's son of the same name was also a surgeon and died at Reddish in 1842 aged 36. Robert Milligan Shipman, a Manchester Attorney and solicitor, lived there in 1856. He moved to Bredbury Hall Stockport and his elder daughter went on to marry a son of Thomas Grundy in 1871.

Archibald Winterbottom, a Manchester and Bradford merchant, resided here in 1861. He later caused a stir in business circles after overcoming a debt of £46,000 in 1882. Grateful creditors organised a dinner in his honour at a hotel in Bradford and presented him with a silver service. The Winterbottom family firm resumed their textile printing business at Newton Street Manchester, and Archibald went to live in Pendleton.

Leopold Samson, a shipping merchant born in Hanover, Germany, moved into the house in about 1864. By 1871 he had moved to Withington, Manchester and was later listed as a calico merchant. Charles Clifton Moore, who died here in 1921, was a chemical engineer who formed his own company after working for Brunner Mond and Co. He was also President of Liverpool Geological Society and published papers on rock analysis. The 1939 directory lists William Tranter MD, physician and surgeon at Reddish House.

Inscribed initials of Edward Stelfox and his wife Elizabeth who lived in Reddish in 1791. The plaque is on a house at the side of Reddish House.

ALSO AT REDDISH HAMLET

1851 - John Harrison, canal agent.
1881- Lieutenant-Colonel Albert H Godfrey, born in St Helier, of the Prince of Wales Volunteer Regiment.
1891- Thomas Bennett Nash, a banker and money changer with premises at Cross St Manchester and the Cattle Market Salford who went bankrupt in 1894 with liabilities of £60,000.

1891- Bythwaite Bond, railway crossing gateman.
1901 - Henry Chauf, manager of a textile warehouse and factory.
1911 - Rev James Pawley, Wesleyan minister; Simeon Heathcote, retired farmer.

WARBURTON

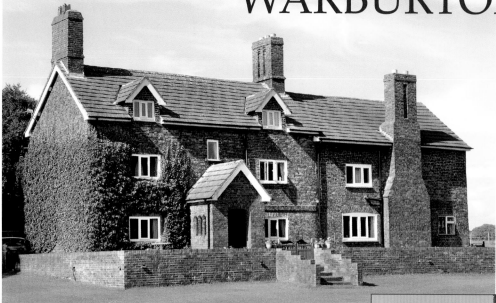

Warburton Park has a Norman mound which had a timber stockade and was surrounded by a moat. Its name derives from the 16th century when deer were kept or hunted within a raised hedge area. The Warburton family lived here at the manor house before they moved to Arley in 1469, although another branch of the family lived here in the 17th century.

The present Park Farm House has a remnant of a wall from the old hall. The pond and brook on the south side are thought to be the remains of the old moat. There used to be a private chapel at the side of the house, but this has been demolished. The chapel bell which used to summon the farm servants for worship has been re-sited outside the rear of the house. There is a tree-covered artificial mound to the east which is an old burial ground.

The old Warburton village pump on Wigsey Lane is shown on the 1928 Ordnance Survey map.

Warburton
High Level Bridge

This replaced the Rixton and Warburton toll bridge over the River Mersey completed in 1866, which linked the Lancashire coalfields with Cheshire, as well as providing opportunities for farmers and traders. The bridge became part of the road up to the new high-level bridge, with the Ship Canal Company taking over the toll rights. The river had been navigable into Manchester but this section of the river was closed and filled in with the coming of the canal.

Above: The bridge under construction over the Manchester Ship Canal September 1892. The section of the River Mersey on the left was later filled in after the opening of the canal.

Below: Bridge span being lifted from the canal September 1892.

Work began on the canal in 1887 and by June 1892 the new bridge was nearing completion with the central girders being put into position. Dredging was continuing, along with work at the junction of the Ship Canal and the River Bollin. The canal narrows to a 90ft width along this section up to Partington, then widens to 120ft. The construction of the canal had involved 16,341 men and boy workers. There had been

Winch at Warburton High Level Bridge September 1892.

Conveyor belt trays at Warburton August 1892 loading extracted material into railway trucks.

over 3000 serious casualties who would have been treated at first-aid stations by the canal or at one of three specially-built hospitals.

Flooding of the workings occurred in 1888 when work stopped and machinery was buried under the mud. The flooding also uncovered variegated strata in the sides of the cutting similar to that found on the Norfolk coast. In April the following year a landslide covered a steam excavator and about twelve wagons, causing £2000 damage. Fortunately it happened during the night otherwise it could have caused many casualties. Heavy rain in November 1890 caused further flooding at the Warburton Cutting which was not cleared until the following March.

The bridge, built on the cantilever principle, weighed 783 tons, with a centre span of 206ft, and a clearance of about 75ft above water level and opened in 1893. This is one of seven fixed bridges designed by Edward Leader Williams the Chief Engineer of the canal. He was also responsible for the impressive Barton Swing Aqueduct and later knighted for his services.

SS Dafila at Warburton Bridge 1929.

Warburton Bridge c1950.

At the Ship Canal's 'unofficial' opening on New Year's Day 1894, huge crowds gathered to watch the procession of boats from Latchford to Manchester Docks. Thousands assembled at Warburton along the canal bank and on the bridge to watch the dignitaries pass by. Many came by train from Manchester and the surrounding area to witness this historic occasion, while others travelled in by horse and carriage or on foot.

The day was bright with a cold wind on what was a public holiday for the district, and a reporter described how it seemed as though the whole countryside was there that day, with Warburton Bridge 'black with the cheering crowds' waving hats and handkerchiefs. It was difficult to see the bridge with so many people packed on it. Either side of the bridge there was a long line of vehicles.

The dredger 'Barry' was moored close to the mouth of the River Bollin and as the procession sailed past the crew of the dredger gave a great cheer then sang 'For he's a jolly good fellow'. Shots were also fired which attracted a lot of attention. It took three hours for the procession of boats to pass by, led by the steam yacht 'The Norseman' carrying the Ship Canal directors. The whole event passed without incident with large numbers of the Lancashire and Cheshire constabulary present. Within a week of the canal's opening, 29 vessels had brought in 27,000 tons of cargo.

SS America, one of the Liverpool Steam Tug Company's six boats in the canal opening procession, carrying nearly 700 passengers.

The toll bridge, sometimes referred to as 'The Bridge of Sighs' because of motorists' frustration at queuing to cross the bridge, initially did not make much money because traffic was sparse. The toll-keepers supplemented their income by running other businesses. Today, tolls are collected from motorists throughout the year, except Christmas Day.

HEATLEY

Bridge over the Bollin for the proposed railway from the Heatley Salt Works towards the Ship Canal.

The Green Dragon at Heatley Heath was for sale in 1795. When it was again sold in 1879, the site included a cottage, a former blacksmith's shop used as a hamper-maker's shop, stabling for four horses, coach house, cow shed, large bowling green and a substantial area of land.

At the time it was occupied by Mr JB Mercer. That same year, the body of a man was recovered nearby from the River Bollin and taken to the Green Dragon to await identification. The deceased was dressed in a dark shooting suit, wore an expensive gold watch, and carried other jewellery, and was later identified as a collector for the Widnes Local Board.

Heatley was the venue for an illegal prize fight in September 1867 between two Manchester catch-weights, Joe 'Rott' Bickerstaff and Joe 'Pudding' Charlesworth. 'Pudding' was on top in the contest with a knock-down but the police arrived within forty minutes and arrested Bickerstaff and some of the spectators. The backers of the two fighters had to agree to a draw. The fight had drawn a large crowd who caused damage to fences and property. The two pugilists were summoned to Lymm Police Court and were charged with a breach of the peace, and several beerhouse keepers and publicans were charged with aiding and abetting. The defendants were bound over to keep the peace for six months and fined 15s costs.

Acknowledgements

With thanks to the following for their invaluable help:

James Allen, Beech Hall School
Dave Birley, birley.org website
John Bowler
Anthea Brough
David Bullock
David and Barbara Bullock
Cheshire Archives and Local Studies
Mike Cooper, Avalon Europe Ltd
Susan Cooper, Wilmslow Historical Society
Tim Emery
Don Foden
Len Grant
Angharad Gwilym, National Trust
John Hambleton
Tim Harding, Bollin Valley Partnership
Ian Harrison, Dean Row Chapel
Chris Hill
Birgitta Hoffman
Cynthia Hollingworth
Emma Houghton, Bollin Valley Partnership
Peter Jackson
Martin James, Bollin Valley Partnership
Michael and Emily Janes
Rev Sharon Jones, Dearnley Parish Church
Dulcie Kelsall, Philip Kelsall, Alex Kelsall
Harmen Koop, United Utilities

John Langdrill, Macclesfield and District Field Club
Joan M Lupton, National Trust
June Mabon, Trafford Ramblers Group
Manchester University Extra Mural Tytherington Study Group
David Miller
Peter McLoughran
George Morgan
Diana G Payne
James Pearson
Joan Pendlebury
Jean Peters
Hazel Pryor
Peter Scott
Wilf Slack
Molly Spink
Keith Smith, Macclesfield Civic Society
Lynn Smith, Lymm History Society
Fiona Swailes, Bollington Civic Society Photo Archive
Trevor Stone
Dr Chris Studds
Ron Thorn, Macclesfield Museums
Alkestis Tslika, National Trust
Chris Tonge
John Twigg
Michael and Kath Walker
Tim Walmsley, Manchester Airport
Paul Walton
Nicola Whyton, National Trust
Alexander and Andrew Wright

My thanks to the archives and local history staff at Chester, Dunham Massey, Macclesfield, Macclesfield Silk Museum, Quarry Bank Mill Styal, Trafford, Warrington, and Wilmslow.

I am grateful to David Bullock, Mavis Timson, David Miller, Chris Hill, Molly Spink and Lynn Smith who checked the manuscript, and also to Pat Gothard, Cynthia Hollingworth and Judith Warrender for their proof checking.

Further information:

A Styal of its Own, by James Stanhope Brown

Altrincham History Society Journal - various

Bowdon Sheaf - various

Archaeological Watching Brief at Hawthorn Hall, by Richard Chatterton & Alex Thornton

Below Manchester, by Keith Warrender

Bollin Valley, From Macclesfield to the Ship Canal, by Keith Warrender

Cheshire at the Opening of the 20th Century, ed by WT Pike

Cheshire Life - various

Cheshire Notes and Queries - various

Doing the Doors, by Robin Barratt

Dunham Massey, Cheshire: a History, ed by Don Bayliss and David Miller

East Cheshire Past and Present, by JP Earwaker

Jackson's Brick Works web site

Warburton Preserved, by Peter Warburton (Cheshire History no 43)

Langley, the History of a Cheshire Village, by Cyril H Dawson

Lindow and the Bog Warriers, by Matthew Hyde and Christine Pemberton

Manchester Airport Second Runway, by Malcolm Pithers (unpublished)

Manchester Astronomical Society website

Manchester to Styal Via Swinton, by James Stanhope Brown

Opening of the Trentabank Reservoir, by Macclesfield Corporation

Over the Hills Near Macclesfield, by Walter Smith

Place Names of Cheshire, by J McN Dodgson

Reservoir Railways of Manchester & the Peak, by Harold D Bowtell

Sanctuary from the Trenches, Stamford Hospital, by Susie Stubbs

Stamford Lodge Wilmslow, a Programme of Archaeological Works, by Alvaro Mora-Ottomano

The First Hundred Years, Dearnley Parish Church, by Gordon Hall

The Quarries of the Macclesfield Area, by DA Kitching

The Sutton St James Story, by Alan Dinnis

The Story of Dean Row Chapel, by Walter H Burgess

Warburton, ed Michael Nevell